Towards practice theory

Library of Social Work

General Editor:
Noel Timms
Professor of Social Work Studies
University of Newcastle upon Tyne

Towards practice theory
Skills and methods in social
assessments

Kathleen Curnock and Pauline Hardiker

Routledge & Kegan Paul
London, Boston and Henley

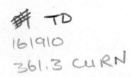
First published in 1979
by Routledge & Kegan Paul Ltd
39 Store Street, London WC1E 7DD,
Broadway House, Newtown Road,
Henley-on-Thames, Oxon RG9 1EN and
9 Park Street, Boston, Mass. 02108, USA
set in 10 on 11pt Times English
and printed in Great Britain by
The Lavenham Press Ltd
Lavenham, Suffolk
© Pauline Hardiker and Kathleen Curnock 1979

British Library Cataloguing in Publication Data

Curnock, Kathleen

Towards practice theory. —(Library of
social work ISSN 0305-4381).
1. Social case work
I. Title II. Hardiker, Pauline
III. Series
361.3   HV43   79-40813

ISBN 0 71000 0338 2
ISBN 0 7100 0339 0 Pbk

Contents

Foreword by Priscilla Young   vii

Acknowledgments   xi

1 **Practice theories and social inquiry assessments**   1

2 **Skills and methods in the acquisition of information**   18

3 **Skills and methods in studying facts and feelings**   39

4 **Skills and methods in formulating an assessment**   57

5 **Skills and methods in setting goals**   73

6 **Assessment processes in different social work settings**   101

7 **Conclusion**   159

Appendices: I, II   173

Bibliography   185

Index   191

Foreword by Priscilla Young

Once upon a time social workers used to talk about study diagnosis and treatment; this was the process to which social workers subjected their clients and one does not have to look far for the model upon which this approach was based. It was assumed that the social worker, like the doctor, had to identify the ills from which his client was suffering, determine the probable cause(s) and the desirable 'cure' and then work with him towards the resolution of his difficulties. In this country, in the 1950s and into the 1960s, such difficulties tended to be defined by qualified social workers in psycho-dynamic terms. In part this was perhaps a reflection of the post-war period of euphoria in which we tended to believe that the Welfare State would protect the individual from the material consequences of his private misfortunes and griefs, and the task of the majority of professional social workers was thus to individualise the public welfare services. The approach was essentially therapeutic, focused on helping the individual client to resolve his personal and internal conflicts, using the professional relationship between client and worker to achieve these aims.

With the growth in studies in sociology, coupled with the dawning realisation that the existence of the 'welfare state' did not eliminate social disadvantage, social workers became increasingly aware that many of the difficulties which their clients presented had their roots in the problems of society, even if they were exacerbated by the psychological problems of the individual concerned. Indeed, some social workers have of recent years perhaps come to feel that their clients' difficulties can be seen only as a reflection of the problems of society, and that the role of a social worker should be to act as an agent of social change.

The authorship of this book has been undertaken by a sociologist and a social worker who have chosen to focus not just on diagnosis, but on the process of assessment as they define it. They have used their combined experience and their different perspectives to analyse the 'practice wisdom' of social workers within the assessment process, and to demonstrate that it has a sufficiently recognisable theoretical base to be regarded as a developing 'practice theory'. This discussion of the process of assessment brings into sharp focus two related areas of current debate in the field of social work; what is social work? and in what terms should it be defined?

Social work appears to be going through a public crisis of identity. The range of functions accruing to the personal social services, together with the very rapid expansion in staff in the 1960s and early 1970s, in the context of major structural re-organisations, have combined not only to confuse employers and the general public about what social work actually is, but also to create a debate within social work itself. The recently published document *The Social Work Task*,[1] studies by local authority employers, and consultations about the expectations of training courses for social workers[2] serve to demonstrate a recognised need to clarify the contribution of professional social work to the personal social services.

In default of any clearer definition, social work tends to be described in terms of the tasks which social workers undertake, and since they form the bulk of field staff in local authorities and in the probation and after-care service, definitions of social work tend to be wide-ranging. This approach fits with the idea of social work humanising and individualising the welfare services, but it does little to identify what the skills of a social worker actually are. Clarification becomes increasingly important since there are many functions which are, or could be carried out just as well or better by staff other than qualified social workers.

It is sometimes argued that no progress will be made until the essence of social work has been distilled, so that it can be studied as a discreet activity, which could presumably be recognised as the same whether carried out in public agencies or in private practice. My own view is that one factor which identifies social work is the context in which it is practised, i.e. a social welfare agency, or an organisation which requires the contribution of social work the better to carry out its own primary function. A hospital is a good example. In other words, I find it difficult to identify social work as a professional activity separate from the functions of an agency. The logic of this view is that although a social worker may indeed be a change agent in many senses, social work as a professional activity cannot be practised in spite of the practitioner being a probation officer, a local authority or voluntary agency employee, but only within that context. Thus I find the approach adopted in this book congenial, and the case studies show clearly the social workers' acceptance and constructive use of their responsibilities as an agent of the organisations for which they work.

None the less, a social worker must also have special skills which are more than common sense or 'practice wisdom', which distinguish him as a qualified professional. If a qualified social worker cannot be so recognised, there is no justification for professional education, as opposed to apprenticeship or in-service training. Theories of practice for social work have been to some degree developed but practice theory is something different. In examining assessment, Kathleen Curnock and Pauline Hardiker have analysed this process in a new way. This is not the old style study/diagnosis process, although elements of it are recognisable, and the authors themselves suggest that some readers might find their approach 'rather conservative'. They describe the process undertaken by the professional social worker who has to recognise that the assessment to be undertaken is for the information of someone else (the court, the doctor, a colleague, the school), who has to make a decision in which the social worker's contribution is only one, if a very important, factor. The 'balance sheet' drawn up in relation to *risks*, needs and resources (my italics) clearly recognises the social worker's responsibility both as a professional person assessing the risks of any recommendation to the personal well being of the client(s) involved, while balancing this against the protection of societal norms. This approach disregards neither the personal internal problems of individuals, nor the ills of society which help to create the problems within individuals; it has no explicit ideological stance, except in its emphasis on individualisation.

A contemporary study of local authority social service area teams[3] reveals that few of the social workers interviewed were able to give any indication that they were consciously applying any theoretical knowledge to their practice, and were rarely able to include in descriptions of their activities the concepts which guided them in carrying out their professional tasks. They seemed to acknowledge the possession of theories of practice to some degree, but were unclear about how (or if) they applied such knowledge, and could not articulate any practice theory.

The authors of this book agree that social workers *do* possess practice theory, derived from both experience and text book knowledge, but that the process of using theory is imperfectly understood. The framework presented for the conceptualising of practice theory in assessment may not be the formulation which everyone would accept, but it demonstrates that there is 'a logical analysis which can be carried through by anyone with a trained mind' (p. 9). One of the aims of professional education is to train social workers in a way that enables them to analyse their own practice, but evidence that this process continues as they gain experience, or that it results in the formulation of practice theory, is not encouraging.

Kathleen Curnock's and Pauline Hardiker's book provides a method of analysis which is valuable in itself, and perhaps even more importantly, they have contributed towards a clearer understanding of the particular skills which the qualified social worker offers.

[1] Working Party on the Social Work Task—BASW, 1977.
[2] Central Council for Education and Training in Social Work—Consultative Document No. 3. 'Expectations of the Teaching of Social Work in Courses Leading to the Certificate of Qualification in Social Work', Reg Wright, 1977.
[3] DHSS—Social Service Teams: *The Practitioner's View*, HMSO, 1978 (p. 133 ff.).

Acknowledgments

During our work for this book we have been helped by many people. It is not possible to name all of them because in so doing we might risk exposing the identities of some of the clients mentioned in the text. We hope that the workers concerned will understand our reasons and be willing to accept a general expression of gratitude for the enormous help that they gave. First we wish to thank all the probation officers in two midlands towns whose ninety social inquiry reports formed the basis of the first project undertaken by Pauline Hardiker. Next we wish to thank the probation officers of the intake team of the larger midlands town whose many reports were monitored by Pauline Hardiker. From these reports we selected information which helped take our thinking further as we struggled to describe the assessment model in inquiry work. The probation officers would not have been able to help us without the willing co-operation of the administrators, and we are grateful to them for making the projects possible, and that this enabled us to undertake our work together for this book. We would also like to thank the Social Science Research Council for funding the two projects.

We think that the opportunity to include detailed accounts of three cases in Chapter six has been an important contribution to the book. We would, therefore, like to thank particularly the three social workers who agreed so willingly to discuss their work with us. They were generous in giving their time and professional knowledge as they talked of their work.

At the School of Social Work, Leicester, we have had much support and encouragement from all colleagues to complete this task we undertook together. We have appreciated their interest and patience. Another source of encouragement to us in our work on assessment has been the interest and questions raised by the students in the school. We realise that they may have had little

Acknowledgments

chance to avoid the subject of social inquiries but we appreciate their many comments which helped us to think more clearly!

Four colleagues, Herschel Prins, Valerie Bean, David Webb and John Haines were especially helpful by reading and commenting on drafts of the book at various stages. Their comments and questions helped us to clarify and review what we wanted to convey.

We should like also to mention four other people who read and made constructive criticisms on the drafts, Professor Noel Timms, Robert and Vicky Tod of Birmingham and Deirdre Flegg, now in the Dorset Probation and Aftercare Service. Philippa Brewster (Routledge) has also been a source of encouragement and help to us.

We have received support and encouragement in our work from Bob Curnock, who also helped with the editing of the final draft of the book.

We wish finally to express our thanks to Sheila Wesson for her invaluable help in typing the manuscript of the book.

Chapter one

Practice theories and social inquiry assessments

Mr John Smith, aged twenty-two, was charged in the magistrates' court with theft of furniture (valued at three hundred pounds) and receiving scrap metal. He had been charged with theft the previous year, when he had been fined. A social inquiry was prepared and the probation officer asked the court to consider placing Mr Smith under supervision, 'so that he can be given guidance and support during this difficult time'. How did the probation officer come to that conclusion? This is the topic we shall explore in this book.

First, a social inquiry was requested because Mr Smith already had a record. Not only had he appeared in court the previous year, he had also appeared before the juvenile court and had been in care as a child. The probation officer interviewed Mr Smith at home, once alone and once with his wife, and he also saw Mr Smith in the office. He had access to previous records relating to the period when Mr Smith was in care and he discussed the case with the social worker who was currently working with the family because the children were considered to be at risk. So, the probation officer had acquired a lot of information from a variety of sources, including his own observations of Mr Smith in the context of his home and family. The following factors seemed relevant:

1 His early childhood had been disrupted when the family moved districts and it was at that time that Mr Smith and his siblings came to the notice of the police, were in trouble at school and were received into care.
2 Mr Smith had several jobs after an uneventful school career but eventually became unemployed due to a serious spinal injury.
3 Mr Smith was married to a divorcée who had three children. The family lived in temporary council accommodation which was in an extremely poor condition. There were outstanding

debts from Mrs Smith's previous marriage but the family was due to be rehoused by the council.

4   The family was poor because of the low income and heavy financial commitments.

5   Information was available about Mr Smith's criminal record and his current offences. His wife was also still paying a fine arising from a shop-lifting offence the previous year.

6   The court would probably take a very serious view of this case especially in the light of Mr Smith's record.

So, a good deal of information had been acquired in this case about Mr Smith's background and his current situation.

Second, what *sense* did the probation officer make of all this information as he studied Mr Smith?

1   There was evidence that Mr Smith had experienced rejection by his parents at the time he was taken into care, but that he responded well to firm and caring control. However, he recalled a happy childhood and a stable family life, claiming his parents were always good to him. On the other hand, the authorities had felt that his parents were inadequate to care for the children.

2   Mr Smith's irregular employment record had added to his insecurity. In particular, 'he tends to react very strongly to rejection and he felt rejected by the firm he had been working for when he damaged his back, because he thought they had not done much for him or taken much interest in or cared for him'.

3   The marriage was apparently happy; the three children had taken to Mr Smith very well and fully accepted him as their father. The social worker confirmed this impression. However, the family lived in extremely poor conditions. This, together with heavy financial commitments, created many pressures for Mr Smith, who felt ashamed of not being able to keep his family in better conditions. He suffered from a loss of masculine pride in this respect.

4   Mr Smith was currently unemployed due to a serious spinal injury and was in receipt of sickness benefits.

5   The current offences were thought to be related to Mr Smith's financial situation. He was finding it very difficult to cope and a friend had suggested that Mr Smith should join him in handling furniture and scrap metal. Though the offences were committed primarily for financial reasons, the probation officer felt there were more complex underlying reasons for them, including Mr Smith's loss of masculine pride and his need to restore this by gaining access to some money. Therefore, the probation officer thought that Mr Smith's offences

were a symptom of his underlying personal problems and a pointer to the need for social work intervention.

6 It was felt that Mr Smith attempted to solve his financial problems by criminal means and that the court would consider it appropriate to help him solve his problems in non-criminal ways. He was considered suitable for probation and there were resources to help him in this respect.

The probation officer studied Mr Smith's case within a 'treatment' framework. This meant that he interpreted the offences as a symptom of the offender's problems related to his background and thought that Mr Smith was probably pushed into crime by circumstances beyond his control, so the offence could be seen as a pointer to the need for social work intervention.

Third, the probation officer drew up a balance sheet in *formulating* his assessment for the court. Four factors in the Smith case were of outstanding relevance to him:

1 His personality was a major factor because I suspected that he is an inadequately developed person. I was suspicious about his ability to sustain a regular job and to provide adequately for his family; I felt his attitudes towards money were suspect. He runs up debts and complains about them but he had made no effort in the past to pay these off.

2 His family was relevant, because I was trying to keep it together to prevent it splitting up, especially because of the three small children.

3 The offence pointed to a man who, in a tight situation, would seize an opportunity with very little thought about the long-term consequences. He was a young man who tended to live from day to day.

4 His economic circumstances were precarious because he was under so many financial pressures.

Each of these factors was an indication to the probation officer of Mr Smith's need for support in order to get back to work eventually, to encourage and help him to pay his debts, and because of the possibility of the family breaking down under these stresses. There was also a risk that Mr Smith might seek criminal means of solving his difficulties if he were not given some help. A probation order seemed an appropriate resource, given Mr Smith's needs and the risk of future offences. The probation officer did not find it difficult to come to this conclusion and made a direct recommendation for probation. A suspended custodial sentence was an alternative possibility but was not seriously considered.

Fourth, the probation officer's *goal* was to ask the court to

3

consider placing Mr Smith under supervision so that he could be given guidance and support at a difficult time in his life. He added that this might also help Mr Smith to avoid attempting to solve his problems in criminal ways in future. The court was also asked to bear in mind Mr Smith's vulnerable financial position if they were considering a fine.

The court gave Mr Smith a three months' prison sentence, suspended for two years, and ordered him to pay restitution. The probation officer thought this was clearly the wrong disposal because he felt that Mr Smith was still vulnerable to commit other offences whilst nothing was being done to support him with his family problems. However, the court gave Mr Smith a 'non-treatment' sentence.

Mr Smith's probation officer acquired a lot of information from a variety of sources, studied it within a treatment framework and formulated an assessment in terms of risks, needs and resources as he set his goal of social work support for this offender.

The knowledge base of social work

The case outlined above illustrates a typical social inquiry situation and the picture will be familiar to most social workers. Mr Smith's circumstances and the probation officer's assessment of them have been documented in a relatively descriptive manner and most readers will probably agree that the recommendation for probation seemed logical and appropriate; given the facts, readers would probably have come to a similar conclusion themselves. But what is it about this case that seems familiar to social workers? Is it because most clients of probation officers and social workers have housing, financial, personal and financial difficulties? Is it because most social workers tend to think that criminal behaviour is tied up with an offender's difficulties? Is it perhaps because social workers find themselves identifying with the probation officer as he made his assessment of Mr Smith? Perhaps some social workers might think that Mr Smith's criminal activities were fairly calculated rather than a symptom of his problems and that it would have been more appropriate to punish him than to offer social work assistance. Alternatively, other social workers might think that it is not surprising that Mr Smith tried to get something for nothing, given his social circumstances and personal experiences; in which case, the social inquiry report might include comment about the normality of his coping mechanisms and the need to protect his rights.

Whatever a social worker's reaction to this particular case, it might be argued that it was experience that led the probation officer to his conclusion. From his work with other offenders, the things which were said in his agency and his observations of the court, he knew that probation was appropriate in this case. Or could that case have been lifted from a text-book on psycho-dynamic casework? The probation officer thought that Mr Smith had experienced 'rejection', was an 'inadequately developed person', was losing his 'masculine pride', and his offences were a 'symptom of his underlying personal problems'. But, however much social workers have to rely on both experience and textbook knowledge in their practice, it may not be very useful to think of these different sources of knowledge as discrete and separate phenomena. Whether knowledge is learned from books or fieldwork activity, it is the *process* of using such knowledge in practice which needs to be understood. Mr Smith's probation officer had to filter a lot of data as he conducted his social inquiry, and he would probably have to integrate his ideas, observations and feelings about the case before he could come to the conclusion that probation seemed appropriate. It is the process of using different types and sources of knowledge in social work practice which will be explored in the book.

Practice theory and the theory of practice

Social workers rely on two types of theory in their social work practice: practice theory and the theory of practice (Evans, 1976). The profession's practice theory is implicit in what social workers do and in how they make sense of their experience. For example, the probation officer selectively perceived and filtered a mass of material about Mr Smith through a particular framework in order to come to an explanation of the situation and to make a decision about what should be done. The particular framework he used is not at all obvious or explicit to us because most of the time he was theorising in a fairly implicit way, but we have interpreted his approach as treatment-oriented. The story that seemed to be emerging was one of a man in difficulties, who was perhaps inadequate and tended to behave thoughtlessly in a tight situation. The probation officer using his social work skills of observation and communication as he weighed up the situation. Similar facts might have told him or another social worker an entirely different story. For example, it might have been thought that Mr Smith had overcome his early background problems now that he was married and had three children who loved him; perhaps he was lucky to have a house, and maybe he and his wife were not helping themselves enough; if she went to work and the couple budgeted more appropriately, some of their difficulties could be dealt with without outside intervention. Clearly, this was not how the probation officer made sense of the facts before him; he was filtering the information he was getting within a framework which told him that the offences were related to Mr Smith's personal and social problems, and that a probation order seemed to be an appropriate source of help.

So whatever theories the probation officer had learned from books, he had to develop a method of using them in his day-to-day work. He probably related to Mr Smith on the basis of certain assumptions about human behaviour. For example, he might think that most people are self-determining except when difficulties overwhelm them. He still had to relate such assumptions to his observations about Mr Smith's life cycle (a young, inadequate, married man with three children), his social circumstances (housing, health, work, family and financial stress), and probation and sentencing rules (a probation order seemed appropriate and resources were available). Furthermore, these practice theories were being used in the context of a professional relationship with a man thought to be in distress. The probation officer therefore relied on more than his experience as he assessed Mr Smith's situation. He was using theories (some of them home-made and common-sense, some of them based on social work principles and social science knowledge) even though these were perhaps relatively implicit, both to him and to us, until we endeavour to make them explicit.

There are two aspects of practice theory which require further elaboration. First, the idea of practice theory helps us to see that social workers are involved in an active process of conceptualisation in their day-to-day work; to describe this as the use of experience underestimates the similarities between the thought process and conceptual struggles we engage in when we work with clients and when we read our books. As Bartlett (1970) argues, assessment is a distinct intellectual process based on knowledge and values. It is a logical analysis which can be carried through by anyone with a trained mind. Social workers' practice theories appear to be based on something more than experience.

Second, the practice theories which social workers carry around in their heads, and which provide them with frameworks by which they can filter a mass of data, come from somewhere. For example, as we have seen, Mr Smith's probation officer used words such as insecurity, ashamed, rejection, inadequate and symptom; he linked Smith's unemployment with his insecurity and thought that his offences were connected with his loss of masculine pride. This seems to suggest that the probation officer was drawing on some kind of psycho-dynamic casework framework to help him to make sense of the case.

Therefore, the idea of practice theory conveys two things. One relates to the active process of conceptualisation required in day-to-day social work practice; the other relates to the frameworks social workers use to help them make sense of the mass of material they must handle. These frameworks may range from psycho-dynamic to sociological theories but they will frequently be of a psycho-social and eclectic nature, including traditional ideas about clients.

Practice theory is sometimes referred to as 'practice wisdom' (Baker, 1975; Bartlett, 1970; Specht, 1977) in social work. For example (see Baker, 1975, p. 200) social work has a lot of information about people in states of stress, systems which do not meet basic human needs and 'know how' about ways of doing things. Unfortunately, much of this 'wisdom' or 'theory' remains at the level of assumptive knowledge because it has not been validated or tested. Perhaps of more importance for the profession is the fact that accumulated wisdom has not been sufficiently formulated into concepts and generalisations so that it cannot be fully shared and passed to future generations (Butrym, 1976). As Evans points out (1976, p. 193), if practice theory is valid knowledge, it should be conceptualised and codified so that it can be incorporated into theories of practice in social work. We do not have access to Mr Smith's probation officer, so he cannot tell us about his practice wisdom. However, if we can explore how he used various sources and types of knowledge as he did his social inquiry, we may be able to incorporate some of our analysis into the practice theories which we shall attempt to conceptualise and codify in this book.

Social workers are sometimes more explicit about some of the theories that they draw on in their practice—they use theories of practice. These refer to the knowledge which is available in a fairly unmodified form from the social and behavioural sciences; but for several reasons, this borrowed knowledge creates problems for the social work profession. First, social workers still have a long way to go in implementing theoretical concepts (for example, learning, roles, social change) developed in the social sciences (Brennan, 1973, p. 7). Secondly, there is rarely a direct link between theoretical concepts and their practical application, because social work has to organise and select its knowledge in the light of its tasks and the people it works with (people in personal and social need). As Butrym (1976) points out, social workers use both deductive and inductive types of knowledge, but we have failed to incorporate this sufficiently into our theories of practice. Theories and concepts need to be put to the test of practice if they are to be modified and validated, and experience gained in practice should be generalised so that it can form the basis of new concepts and theories. Too often, theory is applied mechanically and dogmatically in social work, and there may be too little reflection on the more general meaning of specific instances of practice. If practice wisdom is not utilised, it cannot be incorporated into theories of practice. Third, even when theory is borrowed in a relatively unmodified form, as in behaviour modification which draws explicitly on experimental psychology and learning theory, the problems of application are formidable and include:

> the limitations in the data, principles and theories which constitute contemporary psychology, the inadequate and indirect derivation of knowledge from psychology for treatment purposes and the practical difficulties of converting such knowledge into usable casework techniques. (Jehu, 1972, p.i)

However much a social worker explicitly selects social science theories in his work, his use of such knowledge will be problematical, and the cornerstone of such selection must be its usefulness. This is probably a major reason why theories of practice have been slow to develop in social work.

To return to the case of Mr Smith, did the probation officer seem to be drawing on explicit social science theories or concepts as he made his assessment? There were several stress factors in the offender's situation: housing, finance, health, work and family. Were these largely a consequence of social inequality, deprivation and poverty which are typical of many lower working-class people or were they primarily connected with Mr Smith's inadequate personality? He might have got into difficulties even if his housing, health, financial and family stresses had been removed. Clearly, the probation officer was making connections between Mr Smith's social situation and his personality and opted for a general kind of psycho-dynamic explanation to link them. He did not deny the man's poverty and social stress, but he thought they related to his inadequacy and inappropriate problem-solving behaviour. There seemed to be little evidence that he was using learning theory or sociology in an explicit way. His most explicit knowledge seemed to be based on certain psycho-dynamic casework assumptions about people's coping abilities and problem-solving capacities.

Practice theories are relatively implicit and theories of practice are rather more explicit, but the differences between these two forms of knowledge need to be more precisely identified. First, a theory may seem explicit to an observer even though it is implicit to the practitioner using it. One reason for this may be that with experience a social worker's theories of practice, which have been learned in a relatively explicit way, may become implicitly incorporated into his practice theories. For example, Mr Smith's probation officer had probably learned his psycho-dynamic theories of practice in an explicit way during training, but these had been implicitly incorporated into his practice theories during his experience of working with offenders.

Second, practice theories are not just applied explicit theories of practice. The relationship between theories of practice and practice theories is little understood in social work, but it is likely that practice theories rely on other things besides explicit theories. They probably consist of imagination, intuition and curiosity (Specht, 1977) and combine sensual perception, cognitive comprehension and affective experience (Butrym, 1976). For example, Mr Smith's probation officer probably used some guidelines in his observations of the family, thought about the relevance of Smith's 'inadequate' personality to the offence behaviour and had some feelings of empathy, warmth and like or dislike for that particular person. If we extract the psycho-dynamic theories of practice from the social inquiry assessment, the content of the probation officer's practice theories will not have been exhausted, because social work relies on other sources of knowledge besides explicit theories.

Third, it is the process of using many types of knowledge within a purposeful relationship which forms the kernel of practice theory. The constituent elements of this process cannot be spelled out here, but these are some of the things which will be explored throughout this book. It is possible that the process of using practice theories is similar whether a social worker draws on psycho-dynamic or socio-logical theories of practice. For example, it may be concluded that a person is in need, even if one worker pitches his analysis at the level of the person whilst his colleague locates need in the structure of social relationships (Hardiker and Webb, 1978). Nevertheless, the issue is problematical and remains little understood. Therefore, while a practitioner's theories of practice may become implicit to him with experience, practice theories consist of other forms of knowledge besides theories of practice, and it is the process of using different types of knowledge which needs to be explored.

Unless the knowledge base of social work—implicit or explicit—is scrutinised, it may be indistinguishable from idiosyncratic bias. For example, was Mr Smith at the mercy of the particular probation officer who handled this case? Might another probation officer employing very different theories of practice or practices theories have reached a different assessment? This is always a possibility in any profession and this is one reason why Bean (1975a and 1975b) urges offenders to choose their probation officer with care because, under similar circumstances, one may recommend a fine whilst another may suggest a custodial sentence. However, there is evidence of more similarities than differences between probation officers in this respect (Hardiker, 1977a). But a social worker's particular assumptions about human behaviour—implicit or explicit—will have some bearing on his professional decisions. For example, a probation officer who subscribes to treatment model explanations of delinquency may be more likely to recommend probation rather than custody for an offender (Hardiker, 1977a; Stoll, 1968; Wheeler, 1968). It is debatable whether that probation officer is aware of either the assumptions behind his practice or their implications because such assumptions are rarely made explicit. However, whether they are implicit or explicit, they are still theoretical assumptions. As Briar and Miller (1971) point out, if practitioners think that they should be atheoretical, this really means that they favour implicit and hidden rather than explicit and self-conscious theory. The choice for them is not whether to have a theory, but what theoretical assumptions to hold.

In this section we have drawn a distinction between practice theory and the theory of practice in order to try to overcome the false theory-versus-experience dichotomy. We do not wish to imply that social workers' explicit or implicit theories are adequate, because the knowledge base of any profession is always incomplete. In the face of inadequate knowledge, some practitioners resort either to dogma, paralysis, common sense, or blaming the system; others make the false distinction between theory and experience.

It is our belief that social workers have and use a more systematic knowledge base than they usually acknowledge, but that this is rarely codified or documented. Perhaps practice theories have not been either fashionable or acceptable in the profession, so they remain in social worker's heads and daily activities, rather than finding their way into the literature. This may be one reason why the assessment of Mr Smith makes sense to social workers. It fits in with their day-to-day knowledge and ties in with their own social work practice theories that clients' behaviour is sometimes a presenting symptom of underlying problems. And the process of gathering and studying facts and feelings in order to come to some formulation about an appropriate course of action seems to summarise their own activities in social inquiry assessments. However, such practice theories are rarely documented in this way in the social work literature.

We opened this chapter with a description of John Smith's case, but neither a book nor a theory can rely on evidence from one piece of social inquiry work. This may be one of the reasons why social workers may have been slow to develop and codify either their practice theories or their theories of practice and have concentrated on applying rather than creating new knowledge. Compton and Galaway (1975, p. 54) point out that when social workers discuss their practice knowledge in journals, they often only write about unique, individual situations without attempting to generalise their experiences and connect them with existing knowledge. This may seem a harsh judgment but it does remind us that reciprocal links must be made and maintained between theory and practice on the basis of systematic evidence if social work knowledge is to develop.

It should be possible to tease out the assumptions used implicitly and explicitly by social workers as they work with their clients. This should enable some generalisations to be made about the process of using knowledge in social work practice. For example, if a large number of cases can be analysed, it may be possible to indicate the circumstances in which probation officers tend to be treatment-oriented towards their clients, and to compare these situations with those in which less treatment-oriented ideas such as punishment are used (see Hardiker, 1977a). If practice knowledge can be generated in this way, it may feed back into explicit theories, modifying them in the process. Such generalisations may help us to improve and evaluate social work practice if, for example, situations can be avoided in which clients are let down when their chances of going to prison partly depend on the idiosyncratic bias of their social inquiry writer. Finally, documentation of and generalisations about practice theories may restore the links which should be made between theory and practice—each should draw upon and modify the other in any ongoing process.

We set out below the framework which we shall use to make generalisations about assessment processes and practice theories in social inquiry situations. We hope that this exercise will overcome a recurrent problem in social work; we can read and learn about social science theories because they are written down and codified, but we cannot understand and develop practice theories if we have to rely on picking them up as we go about our social work practice since they are not written down. Such haphazard and implicit learning is bound to be problematical, even though all professional knowledge relies on the practical application and use of implicit and explicit theories. If certain principles of practice can be identified and documented, this may contribute to the knowledge base of the profession and thus to social work practice.

Social inquiry reports and social work assessments

The social inquiry report on Mr Smith was prepared by a probation officer for a magistrates' court. The Powers of the Criminal Courts Act, 1973, outlines the duties of the probation officer in these circumstances:

> to enquire in accordance with any directions of the court, into the circumstances or home surroundings of any person with a view to assisting the court in determining the most suitable method of dealing with his case, ... (Schedule 3, para. 8(1))

It may be thought that social inquiry reports, particularly those prepared by probation officers, are only descriptions of circumstances in accordance with the official definition of their purpose. Indeed, Davies (1974) has argued that this is all that can be validly claimed for social inquiry reports. Even so, the nature of social inquiries seems to be more complex than this for several reasons.

First, accepting even this lowest common denominator—that reports are descriptions of circumstances—begs the question of what counts as a description and of which circumstances are considered. As we have seen in the case of Mr Smith, the probation officer presented a picture of the offender's background and current difficulties. But it can hardly be argued that he was engaged in a simple fact-finding exercise. He was involved in an extremely complex assessment process as he acquired and studied information, weighed up several factors and decided to recommend probation. His social inquiry report told a story, and it is difficult to know whether the court wanted the kind of assistance it received from the probation officer. Even though the sentencers did not follow the probation officer's recommendation, this did not necessarily mean that they were not provided with the relevant information or that they did not take the assessment into account.

Second, the official literature (The Streatfeild Report, 1961; The Morison Report, 1962; Home Office Circular 194/1974) and research evidence (Davies, 1974; Ford, 1972; Perry, 1974; Hardiker, 1975, 1977a, 1977b, 1978) suggest that probation officers are involved in complex and varied roles in their social inquiry work. Sometimes they advise sentencers by presenting either a description of the offender's circumstances or offering a diagnosis and prognosis; in other situations they play a more classical justice role by acknowledging the inevitability of a tariff sentence, given the seriousness of an offence. There are also some cases in which probation officers take a very active role in their social inquiry reports and attempt to manipulate the court into making a 'social work' decision; this usually happens when recommendations are made to keep an offender out of prison. Therefore, if probation officers play a variety of roles in their social inquiry reports and are also active in recommending various sentences, the nature of their activities needs to be explored.

Third, the social work element in social inquiry work remains a controversial issue. Monger (1972) argues that, at least in respect of adult offenders:

the principal objective of a probation officer in carrying out a social inquiry report should not be that of helping the accused with his personal problems, rather it should be that of assisting the court in reaching a decision.

12

Monger takes a rather different view in relation to juvenile offenders (1974, p. 125)

> It is totally unrealistic to enter an enquiry situation unprepared to meet need, to put it on metaphorical ice during the court situation, and then suddenly switch on sensitivity again and expect an instant response from the client.

This is a complex issue because it is not easy to draw a line between a report which assists sentencers and one which is part of a process of helping an offender with his problems. This will probably be so whether the client is a juvenile or an adult. We shall explore this problem by suggesting that there are common social work features in all types of social inquiry work, whether this is done in probation, social services or hospital settings. There are basic social work principles, skills and knowledge which are relevant whether a social worker is preparing a guardian *ad litem,* divorce court welfare, care proceedings, hospital or probation report. The common elements in the process will be examined in terms of social work models developed by Haines (1975) and Compton and Galaway (1975):

Model of Social Work Processes

Haines	Compton and Galaway
	Assessment
Acquisition of information Studying facts and feelings	Problem identification and definition; Goal identification; preliminary contract; Exploration and investigation
Formulation of assessment Goal-setting	Contract phase; assessment and evaluation; formulation of a plan of action; prognosis

Social inquiry ends

— —

Intervention

Evaluation

It can be seen from these models that the primary focus of assessment in social work is on the acquisition and study of information in order to define the problem, and the formulation of an assessment in order to make contracts and set goals. There are similarities between Haines's and Compton and Galaway's models and we shall explore our theme in relation to Haines's version: Assessments in social inquiries will be examined by looking at four phases in the process:

acquisition of information
studying facts and feelings
formulation of an assessment
goal setting

These models help us to identify another important feature of social inquiries—they belong primarily to the assessment phase of the social work process. This has implications because of the audience and function of social inquiry reports, and in respect of social work theories about the uniqueness of the assessment phase of the process.

First, social inquiry reports are usually prepared for another agency or professional, such as a court, lawyer, or doctor. This means that, whatever long-term intervention plans may be identified at the assessment stage, there is neither a contract nor legitimation for them until after a decision has been made by another party such as magistrates or doctors. Consequently, the contracting and goal-setting engaged in by a social worker and his client must focus on the other parties to the contract. For example, probation may be recommended but the offender is fined or sent to prison; alternatively, a court may make a probation order when it has been neither agreed to by the offender at the inquiry stage nor recommended by the probation officer. If the probation officer had initiated an intervention or treatment plan with Mr Smith, there would have been no sanction to continue with it after the court decision of a suspended custodial sentence. Similarly, courts do not always make care orders which have been recommended by social workers, nor do doctors always follow the implications of a social assessment in their discharge policies. (We realise that our argument here is too simple, but it sets the scene for our discussion and we shall return to it in the concluding chapter.) The main purpose of social inquiry reports is to provide an assessment for another professional or agency. The social work element in the process must allow for the third party in the triangle. Therefore, the main purpose of assessment and goal-setting at this stage in the process must be in relation to that other party, and an agreed recommendation may be one part of the process.

Second, not all social work theorists maintain such a sharp distinction between assessment and intervention as we have done. Assessment has been an important topic in the social casework literature (Hollis, 1965; Perlman, 1956; Sainsbury, 1970). Whether the stress has been on social investigation and evidence (Richmond, 1917) or on the special nature of the casework relationship (Ferard and Hunnybun, 1962; Yelloly, 1972), most writers have argued that social workers cannot divorce the assessment from considerations

14

of future help and that the assessment process itself may help the client. For example, when an assessment for material help is made, the client himself may come to some understanding about the sources of his difficulties and begin to do something about them before the assessment is completed. Similarly, family communication problems which might have a bearing on a juvenile offender's delinquency may be resolved during a social inquiry. However valid these arguments are, this book is based on rather different assumptions. A lot of the casework literature is based on psycho-dynamic theory which ascribes particular qualities of insight, empathy, warmth and non-verbal communication to interpersonal processes. The assessment relationship itself must have very special qualities given such psycho-dynamic assumptions. The model used in this book is not based on such assumptions, and an analytical distinction is made between assessment and intervention processes in social work.

Third, if an analytical distinction is made between the assessment and intervention phases of the social work process, this helps us to identify some of the special characteristics of social inquiry work. Whatever the setting, the social work relationship has a specific context, boundary and purpose. The context will relate to agency setting—social services, probation, hospital. The boundary is provided by the purpose of the report—to provide an assessment for another agency or professional. The fact that a social inquiry report is primarily a social work assessment implies that its main focus should be on a problem-definition, a conclusion about appropriate intervention, and therefore a goal in terms of a court hearing, professional decision or recommendation. Assessment is a complex process, but it has an identifiable context, boundary and purpose in social inquiry work. One means of clarifying this is to make clear, analytical distinctions between the assessment and intervention stages of the social work process.

Fourth, even though we have argued that assessment and intervention can be seen as analytically separate phases in the social work process, they cannot be so neatly divided empirically. There are several reasons for this. First, social workers often intervene in a circumscribed way during social inquiry work; at the very least, they will have made some kind of relationship with a client, but they might also have responded to the immediate needs of a client, especially when practical help is required. Second, a stress situation is sometimes identified during a social inquiry, and crisis intervention takes place at this stage. Some writers (Dobson, 1976; Hofstad, 1977; Monger, 1974; Vaisey, 1976; Waters, 1976) have suggested that social workers should capitalise on this; if crisis or task-centred work can be done at the social inquiry stage, either a conditional

15

discharge or a short period of supervision can be recommended. Third, sometimes social workers have to intervene in order to complete their assessment, as when an offender is placed in a bail hostel or community home during the social inquiry period. These are perfectly acceptable activities, provided the probation officer and his client are clear about the limited and specific nature of the intervention at this stage. However, if intervention starts before either an adequate assessment has been made or no agreement has been reached about the nature of the problem, difficulties are likely to arise. For example practical solutions may be inappropriately sought for emotional problems (Jordan, 1972), or psychological help may be offered when the 'real' need is financial (Handler, 1973; Mayer and Timms, 1970).

Social inquiry reports are prepared by social workers in a variety of settings and not just by probation officers. Their content and purpose remain controversial issues, but it can be argued that the social work assessment is an important element in them. We have presented a model of social work processes which makes an analytical distinction between assessment and intervention, and this should enable us to explore some principles of social work practice in social inquiry work.

The focus of this book

The case of Mr Smith was one of ninety social inquiry reports which were analysed as part of a sociological project (Hardiker, 1975)*. As we remarked earlier, neither a theory nor a book can be based on one piece of social work practice and one of the obstacles to building up social work knowledge may have been that social workers have tended to generalise from isolated cases. However, if social work principles can be explored in relation to a relatively large sample of cases, this may enable us to identify some practice theories. Social inquiry reports are a useful medium for this purpose, because they belong to an identifiable phase in the social work process— assessment—and they cross the boundaries of social work settings.

We started this chapter with a probation case, but we opened out our discussion into social inquiry reports in other settings too. This is the method we shall adopt in the book as a whole. Because we have systematic evidence on ninety social inquiry reports prepared by probation officers, we shall explore assessment processes in relation to these first. The logic of our assessment model will be

* Whilst we were preparing this book, we were simultaneously monitoring a probation intake team (Hardiker, 1977b), and we have also used some evidence from that study.

explored by examining a number of cases in which probation officers acquired and studied information, formulated an assessment and set goals in their social inquiry reports. We shall then explore the same processes in relation to social inquiries in other settings: a non-accidental injury in a social services department, a behavioural problem in a child treatment research unit, and a terminally-ill patient in a hospital (Chapter six). Then in the final chapter we shall make some generalisations about practice theories in social inquiry reports.

The illustrations used throughout this book are taken from transcripts of tape-recorded interviews with probation officers and social workers (see Appendix I for an example of the interview schedule used) about particular social inquiry reports. The over-all format we shall use is to make a general statement about the assessment issue in question, to introduce brief details of the case to which reference is being made, then to present the probation officer's or social worker's reasons for coming to the conclusion he did. Though the main body of the book contains illustrations from probation officers' social inquiry reports, our book has relevance for all social workers. We are exploring a variety of social inquiry situations in relation to a model of assessment processes; in the course of this, we are trying to make explicit some of the elements of practice theory on which the practitioners seem to be relying.

Chapter two

Skills and methods in the acquisition of information

The focus of social inquiry work concerned with offenders is the collection of information for the court. The nature and purpose of the information gathered and presented are, of course, critical issues in the literature. Even so, the model we have adopted in this book is based on the assumption that social work processes are basic to all social inquiry work; it is for this reason that professional skill is required in gathering information for the report. This task is more than a fact-finding exercise or administrative procedure, because it calls for an ability to conceptualise and to relate to a variety of people in a purposeful, caring, open and authoritative manner. The skills lie in combining disciplined thought with appropriate relationships in a purposeful task.

Frameworks

The evidence indicates that probation officers work within a particular framework as they gather information for the court (see Hardiker, 1975; 1977b). Typically, they seek data about the following factors when they prepare reports for the criminal courts: the offence and circumstances and the offender's previous criminal record; the offender's family, personality, neighbourhood, economic, health and social circumstances; the sentencing policy of the court and the policy and resources of the probation agency. Such a list indicates nothing about the process of acquiring information but it illustrates that probation officers focus their inquiries on the immediate referral issue: the *offence(s)*, the *offender* before them, and the organisational *setting* in which they must work—the court and the agency. Immediately, it is apparent that there will be boundaries to their investigations within which there may be a relatively wide brief to provide the sentencers with relevant data. We shall examine in later chapters some of the ways in which facts and feelings are studied, but our immediate task is to indicate some of the skills required in gathering information. This early phase of the assessment process has profound consequences for future work with offenders. Failure at this stage of a social inquiry assessment will make it difficult later to define the problem, objectives and goals for the court. It is therefore necessary to spell out the skills required in some detail. There will always be boundaries to a social work interview—the main tool for data collection—depending on the court and agency setting, the purpose for which the report is being prepared, and the respective roles of the client and the worker.

The interview is the main vehicle for collecting information and it has to be planned and arranged in such a way that the optimum use can be made of it; when it is terminated both client and worker should be aware of why it ended there. Many people who have participated in interviews as students and inexperienced social workers can recall with discomfort the feeling of being ill-prepared for starting an interview. Equally painful is the memory of interviews which seemed to continue because there seemed no way of bringing them to a close. The worker will obtain data from other sources too, such as the court referral note and existing agency records, and great skill is needed in using such data appropriately. But we shall focus our discussion on the characteristics of social inquiry interviews, some sources of difficulty and ways in which these may be handled.

Preparation for first contacts

The starting point for the social worker is the request from a court for information about a particular offender—his personal and social circumstances in relation to his offence and possible future sentence.

Purpose of the inquiry

A social inquiry has a specific focus and is not the same as either a casework assessment or the beginning of long-term intervention. There are similarities and many of the same social work skills are needed in all three types of work but the overriding purpose is to gather information to assist others to make a decision. For example, in the case of an offender, the document may be used in either mitigating a sentence (size of fine) or selecting a rehabilitative measure (probation instead of borstal training). Sentencers will want in particular to know if the offender is under stress and in need of social work help. In a divorce court case, the inquiry will be relevant to custody and access decisions and therefore information

19

about parental attitudes and child care will be crucial. In a non-accidental injury situation, the inquiry will relate to decisions about whether a child should be taken into care, so details of family structure and functioning will be vital. The purpose of the report thus becomes a focus for all the inquiry work, though this does not amount to a straitjacket for the worker, who has some professional autonomy in these circumstances.

The purpose of the inquiry will also affect the amount of information the client will need from the worker. In criminal inquiries the worker is responsible for ensuring that the offender knows about the court's choice of disposal and the function of the social inquiry. In a custody inquiry, the court papers may indicate the available choices for future living arrangements. The client needs to know whether the worker is exploring possibilities or assessing the choices already available in respect of a child's future living arrangements.

Information available

The written information available to the worker before he begins his inquiries may vary in different cases, and this has implications for how it should be interpreted and used. In the case of a social inquiry being prepared on an offender known to the agency, careful consideration must be given to the significance attached to the material available in agency records. The current offence may be similar to previous ones and reflect continuing problems or it may be of a different nature and indicate a change of circumstances. Existing records may be used as a source of clues for the worker as he begins to build up hypotheses, but they should not influence him to such an extent that he prejudges the issue. Every social inquiry provides an opportunity for a new look to be given to a case.

The court may make a considerable amount of information available to the worker in a divorce court welfare inquiry. Some of this material may be in legal documents such as affidavits which refer primarily to the parties as marriage partners rather than as parents. These should not be confused with social workers' records. Information in affidavits has been prepared for use in relation to the partners' application to the court for a judicial decision about marriage. It might provide clues about the atmosphere in which a child has lived and provide pointers for the interview with all the partners. Even so, the social worker will need to ask many other questions in relation to decisions which will have to be made about the future care of the child. Information will vary in its meaning, relevance and adequacy according to the purpose for which it was prepared and presented.

20

The referral information the worker receives assists him to prepare for the first interview. He should use this information imaginatively rather than seeking lots of information before seeing the client. For example, the address of the client may indicate stressful housing conditions; the age and family composition of a client's parents may also suggest problematical living arrangements, such as co-residence with in-laws, an unplanned pregnancy or poverty. When a record or report from within the agency is used, the worker must consider carefully how relevant that information is to the current problem. An old record may provide a glimpse of a client's previous life, but it may be only of limited relevance in the current situation; on the other hand it may be an important starting point for first interviews.

The worker begins to hypothesise and speculate in order to prepare possible approaches for the first interview. He starts to compile a list of subject areas to be spanned in discussion. Such a list cannot be completed until the inquiry is well under way and the worker is reasonably satisfied that relevant areas have been covered. The purpose of the inquiry remains the overriding consideration but the preparatory stage of work illustrates the importance of hypothesis-testing in social work. The skill required of the worker lies in the ability to combine disciplined thought, based on knowledge drawn from social science and social work theory, with his own experience and with the use of himself, in an open and flexible way appropriate to the client and the circumstances which the worker faces.

Thoughts and feelings of clients: some possibilities

One of the things the worker may speculate about is the possible reactions of the client in the first interview (Keith-Lucas, 1972). For example, an offender may think the worker can 'do things to him', such as send him to prison or force him to say things he would rather not say. He may expect to discuss the offence and view this prospect with relief or resentment. He may be confused as to why he should be asked very personal questions. In a divorce court welfare inquiry, a parent may see the worker as someone who can be won over as an ally in order to gain custody of his child. Accordingly, he may present a distorted image of his goodness and acceptability as a parent. Even so, the parent may have very mixed feelings of anti-climax, anger, depression, rejection and frustration surrounding the divorce; these feelings will not be very far from the surface as he tries to present himself as a competent, caring and capable parent. Another reaction to the inquiry may be that the parent considers that he has a right to the child and that the court should not challenge this. His attitude to the interviewer may then be one of justifiable annoyance that his mode of life, behaviour towards his child and ability to manage his affairs are being scrutinised. On the other hand he may feel pleased and relieved about the opportunities afforded by a court inquiry. Sometimes the worker may respond with action to the clues he obtains from the brief particulars in the referral information. In one example, the probation officer called immediately on a family in which two children had been referred from the juvenile court earlier that day for reports. A colleague's note to him included comment about apparent tension and distress of the children and the mother. As he decided to go to the house he was aware that he might be coolly received and if that occurred he would merely make a future appointment. In fact, his arrival was seen as an offer of immediate counsel and help in a crisis situation.

Another example illustrates the importance of responding to clues obtained prior to contact with the client. Both these examples also demonstrate that if the worker reaches out to the client in a positive way this is recognised by the person in need. A probation officer obtained no response to two requests she made by letter for a middle-aged woman, accused of shop-lifting, to come to the office so that the report could be prepared for the court. The officer reflected on possible reasons—an unwillingness to co-operate, denial of the offence, anger at the police, the court and the probation service—but inquiries about the offence from the police suggested that the client was uneasy in talking to people in authority. When the worker called on the woman at home (after giving her a further choice about the venue of the meeting) she found a frightened, unsophisticated client who needed and wished for help to explain her circumstances.

Both examples show the worker's preparedness to respond to what is found in the first interview, but approaching it with certain ideas which have been influenced by knowledge and experience but also by the particular clues obtained about the individual case.

The worker's response to information

The social worker's response to the information received through the notification is also an important factor to consider in preparations for first interviews. Data about the offence may indicate either a hasty response to a situation, or a calculated risk, or a 'cry for help' by someone in need. Similarly, the offence may be unusual, or typical of either a particular age group, locality or fashion. Such indications become a source of hypotheses rather than an invitation to stereotype, label or enter a situation with a closed mind. The worker's personal reactions are relevant on many counts. As we have seen, he may treat the initial referral information as a source of hypotheses, but he will also have personal feelings about such things as the nature of the offence. For example, a man was charged with two offences of incest with his young daughter. The probation officer commented that her reactions to the offence were mixed:

> Obviously, my gut reaction was one of distaste really. I do not think my feelings are anywhere near as strong as some, as I think some people are totally disgusted by the idea of incest. But I have probably had enough contact with people who have been involved in it not to be moralistic about it. I think my main concern was what it had done to the girl emotionally, especially in view of her age.

It is clearly important for workers to be aware of their own responses to particular offences. Even so the worker must find out from the offender as much as he can about his perception of the situation and see the offence in the context of his life situation.

The worker has also to examine his reactions in a divorce court welfare inquiry. There may be a fairly substantial amount of written material available to the social worker before the first interview. He has to study that information with a view to separating where possible what it tells him about the person's ability to be a caring parent from the problems that have been evident as a marital partner. He prepares himself to go into the interview knowing that he has to try to make sense of what he sees and is told by that person about himself, his way of life, his attitude to past, current and possible future events, since all these aspects affect the child who is the focus of the inquiry. The worker is likely to have more time than in the inquiry for the criminal court and he plans how to use that time to negotiate his relationship with the persons concerned in the child's life, how he can gain their confidence so that they can be relatively open with him rather than revealing only the aspects of themselves that they think he wishes to see. He aims from the beginning to put the pieces together over a period of time. Throughout his inquiry he bears in mind that the primary concern both he and the court have is the welfare of the child, and he gears his work to this end.

It is therefore important for the social worker to examine and anticipate his own reactions to an inquiry situation as he prepares to set up his first interview and to alter his preconceptions where necessary and as the facts and feelings in the case become clearer to him.

Some guidelines

Compton and Galaway (1975, p. 278) have suggested some guidelines for data collection and we shall discuss these in relation to the inquiry carried out by John Smith's probation officer.

(a)   In a social inquiry situation the offender should be the primary source of information. His offence and the circumstances are the focus for the inquiry and make the offender an indispensable and relevant source of data. In the case of John Smith the probation officer had several sources of information but there is evidence that he used the client as the main source. In the court report the information given about his early background was presented first as Mr Smith remembered it at the time the inquiry was undertaken. The officer indicated also the information available to him from past records. Although there was some discrepancy in the two views, some significance was attached to the client's memory of the past. Information about his current housing, health and family circumstances was obtained first from Mr Smith, then linked with the offender's own observations of these factors and finally confirmed by contact with other relevant sources of information, the housing department , the family doctor and a social worker familiar with the family.

(b)   The data collected in social inquiries must be relevant to the problem being handled. The areas covered during interviews may be far-ranging, but a probation officer goes beyond the bounds of his professional responsibilities if he does not keep firmly in mind the rule that the data collected should be relevant and useful for sentencers. In the case of John Smith, the officer knew that the offence would be viewed as serious by the court. He needed therefore to know the details, and obtained these from the client. The account the client gave indicated full awareness of the possible consequences of his actions, but a preparedness to take a risk which had then misfired for him when the offence was detected. He made no excuse for his involvement in the offence. The officer saw as relevant to the court in making its decision the current home circumstances, health and financial problems which surrounded Mr Smith both at the time of the offence and as he appeared in court. The officer's selection of the necessary amount of detail about any of these factors was guided by the professional responsibility he carried in relation to the task he undertook for his recommendation to the court. In his interviews with the client and others in the environment he could have pursued at greater length factors which indicated questions for him as a social worker who might be involved in continuing work after the court appearance, but to have done so at that stage of contact with the client and his family was not pertinent to his current professional purpose. An exception to this may be when the worker finds a crisis that prevents the client from focusing on the information that the worker requires because of the strong feelings that the crisis arouses in the clients. For example, if the inquiry is concerned with a child who has committed an offence but the parents are distracted from thinking about that because of their current marital crisis, the attention must be paid to that before one can get at the information required about the child's offending behaviour.

(c) The probation officer should not seek information that he would not be willing to share with the client. One might question how the worker is to know what he can or cannot share with the client when he sets about obtaining information. This is a complex issue because professional work involves the ability to share the processes of assessment with the client in order to check its validity and reliability as well as to demonstrate respect for the client. By feeding back to the client information obtained from other sources in order to obtain the client's view about it, the worker reinforces the client as the primary source of information. The worker has the responsibility to find out whether or not the client agrees with what other sources state about him or his circumstances, and should be prepared to express his opinion to the client about the information particularly where the views being given appear to differ.

In the case of John Smith, information from the previous records indicated a quality of childhood experience very different from the client's memory of his childhood. There was less discrepancy between the records and what the client said about the factual events in his childhood. The probation officer may have had more confidence in the accuracy of the contemporary reports about the reasons for the client being removed as a child from his parents, but it was essential that he sought the client's current view of those past events.

Sometimes there is a need to collect information for which the offender might not give permission, as for example, the need to have a psychiatric or medical opinion. In these circumstances it is even more important for the worker to inform the client of his intention and to report to the client on the information he gathers, within the limits of inter-professional confidentiality.

(d) When an assessment or inquiry is begun, the worker should share with the client the information that he already has about the particular problem that has been referred, before the client's thoughts and feelings about it are sought. Otherwise, he may trap the client, who then has either to defend himself against, or collude with, the worker's definition of the problem and this may be entirely inappropriate. We would like to refer here to an example we discuss at length in Chapter six where, during the first interview with the parents over a non-accidental injury referral, the social worker told them in careful detail what she had already found out, how serious she considered the problem to be and the options available. Before she asked for their interpretation of events she explained their rights to them, the steps they may wish to take, what she would be doing and the possible outcomes.

There are boundaries and opportunities in any data-collection exercise for a social inquiry report. The social worker does not go in with a closed mind but has certain hypotheses to follow and definite information to gather for a specific purpose which she will communicate to the client. The guidelines we have suggested should enable the interviewer to fulfil her task in a creative and purposeful manner: use the client as the primary source of information, collect the data for a specific purpose, share the data which has been collected with the client and enable even involuntary clients to be as self-determining as possible. After considering the boundaries and opportunities in any data-collection exercise for a social inquiry report, we turn to the setting in which interviews take place.

Choices and limits of the interview setting

Sometimes, social workers have only limited choices about where they meet the client for the first time. For example, an offender may be remanded in custody for reports or a patient may be bed-ridden in hospital and the interview location is then set for the worker. It is even more important to remember that impressions gained of a person in a custodial setting may be quite false. As one probation officer commented, she found it very difficult to get a clear picture of a man she interviewed in prison because in that context he came over as quiet, rational and calm, but his wife said he was a very unpredictable, violent, aggressive man. The important point about this example is that the probation officer was aware that false impressions may be gathered from interviews in custodial settings and that she had to check out facts and impressions from the man's wife at home. In contrast, the fact that a client has to be interviewed in a hospital bed may help a social worker to gather relevant data. For example, it can provide a very private context on a busy ward and create some informality for the discussion. At other times the bustle of the ward seems to intrude into the discussion. The worker has to be able to respond to the institutional limits in the most appropriate way to enable the client to communicate with him.
  Whenever possible, the client's wishes should be taken into account when arranging the first interview because some offenders do not wish to be interviewed at home. Most social inquiry interviews

will take place either in the office or the offender's home. It is particularly important to try to arrange home interviews in the case of juvenile offenders or in custody and access inquiries, when one focus of work is the decision about the child's future home. In the latter it is important for the social worker to see as much as he can of the child's environment in the time available. This may mean several visits to more than one home when there are contending parents and other adults concerned in the child's life.

Normal social courtesies are as basic to social work practice as they are to other human encounters. Whether interviews take place in a person's home, an office or an institution, time preferences should be respected, suitable introductions made and due allowance made for privacy and uninterrupted discussion. In an institutional setting if interruptions occur, either because of surveillance or normal activity of other people around, the worker should demonstrate his awareness of the effect these have for the client.

The social worker has some choice in an office interview about how much formality to create and seating arrangements are important. Usually, formality and authority are sufficiently indicated by the office setting and it is therefore important to create an open atmosphere for the inquiry interview. Office interviews with children or adolescents may be particularly difficult. Sometimes this may be due to the young person's inability to express himself or because he really does not know what he wants to say. Sometimes it may be because the office setting recalls for the child similar situations where he has been 'summoned' to the presence of an adult. Not infrequently it may be because the youngster is unused to sitting down with an adult and being, for a time, the sole focus of attention. Whatever the reason, the worker has to find ways of enabling the child to respond and talk about himself. Sometimes this is best done through using things like books, games, pencils and paper, or tape recorders as a means of directing attention away from the child and creating space and distance between him and the adult. It is essential for the interviewer to be aware of the ethics of communication in all settings but especially in these difficult situations. He walks a tightrope by enabling the client to say what can be said whilst not tricking him into revealing things he would rather not.

In interviews in home settings, the social worker has to respond to his surroundings and enable the client and others to give the information sought and to express their feelings appropriately. He must be sensitive and responsive to the individual style of verbal and non-verbal communication, especially in family situations (Satir, 1967). The way he handles information may establish a more open atmosphere. For example, he may 'think aloud' about his thoughts and observations in order to create a climate in which the client will

27

feel comfortable enough to share relevant facts and feelings about his situation (Walrond-Skinner, 1976). A social work student re-counted the following incident during the assessment stage of work with a family referred because of their young child's behavioural difficulties.

> The first interview was with the mother, and the child was present, creating chaos all round . . . . My second interview, again in the home, was in order to talk to both parents.
> The husband was very critical of the wife's ability to handle the little girl and look after the house. The more he grumbled, the more the child shouted and tried to get attention from the parents, eventually demanding that he go and get her an ice lolly. He jumped up and rushed off to the shop nearby. On his return I commented that the child had seemed to me to stop the argument between her mother and father by diverting him to the shop. I also commented that maybe when the adults around her shouted to get heard then this may lead Mary to do so. I said I would like to suggest that we tried to talk more calmly to each other as I had felt that I too had begun to raise my voice to be heard above Mary, that in fact she seemed to be 'bossing' us all. The child looked at me and her parents and then came to sit beside me. She was restless at first and then came closer. She was quiet as we talked and seemed more relaxed. The father said, 'You have a way with her'. This gave me the chance to begin to ask both of them about the sort of parents they would like to be . . .

We have stressed the importance of seeing the client as the main source of information and in inquiries concerned with adults one always starts from that premise. The process of the inquiry however may include some interviews with the client and spouse and some with other family household members. It may become clear in the course of the inquiry that if future social work occurs then it will be on a family rather than on an individual basis or may be a combination of both. Where the client is a child or young person and where he is said to have offended, he needs to be seen within the context of his home and family but also as an individual in his own right. In inquiries concerned with very young children, as for instance in non-accidental injury cases or custody inquiries, the worker has to act always in the child's interests and obtain from him what information is appropriate for his age. For example, the only facts that a baby can tell the worker is what the latter can obtain through observation of the child, through watching him with others and their attitude to him and about him. The worker may handle him to feel his responsiveness or lack of it, and will contrive to find out about him from others in the environment. However small a child is, if he is the subject of an inquiry, it is crucial to see him in his home with the people who live with him daily. Sometimes, in addition to seeing the client in the office setting, it may be useful to see other members of the family. The purpose of such an interview and the involvement of others must be clear.

The central aspect of interviews is that two or more people are communicating with each other, so that meanings can be given, received and checked. The meaning of the information acquired and shared will always be bounded given the purpose for which it is being gathered.

Communication

The interview is a specialised form of communication, which has boundaries related to its context and purpose. Because of this, blocks may occur in the communication between the clients and the social worker, who in turn has skills and knowledge which may help him to overcome some of these barriers. Some of the skills required in these circumstances will now be examined.

Boundaries

Context

The context of the criminal social inquiry relates to the court's request for information which will help them in sentencing. The current offence and impending sentence in court thus provide the context for the interview. This provides a limit to what will be shared even when the client may wish to present information that is extraneous to this particular context. The worker has to be clear in expressing to the client what can be included in their visit or what must be left to another time.

Essentials to be conveyed to clients

Because a social worker may have carried out many previous court inquiries, he must not assume that the client is equally clear about the purpose of his inquiry. Each time he begins a new inquiry, it is the worker's responsibility to clarify its purpose to the client so that there is sufficient understanding between them. Sometimes it is difficult, particularly perhaps for less experienced workers, to go into a situation where there is likely to be resentment because someone else (whether it be a court or some other person) has said that there may be a problem. Unless the worker makes explicit to the client why he is there, what his agency (or the court) can do and the focus for their contact, he is likely to have less response and the effectiveness of his efforts can only be reduced.

If the worker and client clarify the purpose of their encounter, they will understand what needs to be shared and the scope of their discussion. Sometimes the worker may ask a question which seems irrelevant on the surface, or the client may provide information which does not appear to be connected to their purpose. It is the worker's responsibility constantly to check out that the purpose of the discussion is understood and to make the appropriate links between the questions asked and information required.

Management and focus of the interview

An interview should be more than a casual exchange of information or an informal conversation and there must be a direction to it. The worker will need to direct the discussion towards securing relevant information for the inquiry whilst at the same time ensuring that the client does not feel bulldozed by an investigating agent. Sensitive listening and purposive responsive comment helps to focus and manage the interview.

Restrictions and resources

Worker and client have specialised roles in an inquiry interview, even if they have been working closely together under a previous supervision order. The worker has a responsibility to use his own personality to create an appropriate distance between them. Probation officers quite often have to prepare a report on offenders already under supervision. In these circumstances the worker has to keep within the role of inquiry agent for the court appearance for a particular offence. He may not want to emphasise the role of worker with a well-known client because that relationship might lead the client to feel he could disclose more than is appropriate to the inquiry. He has to use his knowledge of the offender and his current circumstances relevantly for the purposes of the inquiry.

Specialised roles

The expectations of the social worker's role will facilitate the social inquiry (Perlman, 1968; Ruddock, 1969). The social worker brings his resources of skill, experience, knowledge and personality within the context of what his agency can offer. Even the new social worker starting his first interview has these behind him. Similarly, the role of a client carries responsibilities and privileges: a responsibility to participate in a purposeful discussion and the privilege of not disclosing everything about himself and his situation; in some circumstances, this may go as far as refusing to have a social inquiry prepared on him. In some circumstances the worker needs to feel professionally secure enough to accept the specific role of being a listener and a person who can communicate understanding through attention and physical contact without necessarily using words. He has to be able to demonstrate his competence by listening and feeding back to the client what he hears him saying in order to gain the client's confidence that as a worker, he will play his role appropriately.

In addition to the boundaries to communication that have been indicated there are also barriers, and some of these will now be examined.

Barriers

Communication is always a complex process but some of the sources of barriers are identifiable, and an understanding of these should help the social worker to communicate better in inquiry situations.

The worker and his expectations

If the worker has too tight an expectation of what he thinks the client is going to say and how he is going to respond, it is likely that he will hear only what he is expecting to be told and will not pick up other facts and feelings which the client is trying to convey. Accordingly, he may be unable to respond to, comment on, question or develop ideas the client may be wishing to share. This particular barrier to communication may be evident in interviews with children (Holgate, 1972). For example, the worker may anticipate that a child would rather not discuss a matter which is painful to him, whereas the child may be glad of the chance to share his feelings with an adult who can listen to him. The social worker must remain aware that it is the client's comfort rather than his own which should determine whether or not painful subjects are discussed. When discussing with children either illness or problems between family members it often emerges that youngsters have wanted to ask questions or express anxieties or feelings of anger or guilt, and welcome the chance to clarify their position. The worker needs first to create the climate in which the person, child or adult, can express himself, and must beware of assuming that he knows what the client feels about his circumstances or wants to say about them.

Messages and their meaning

Sometimes social workers receive a message from a client which is not entirely clear, yet they take for granted one possible meaning without checking other possibilities with the client. Unclear messages may arise for a variety of reasons. Sometimes the verbal message itself is unclear; this may happen if a client has a speech impediment, speaks in a strong dialect or talks about things of which the social worker has never heard. In other situations the verbal messages may be contradicted either by gesture, facial expression or tone of voice. Sometimes this discrepancy can be particularly obvious to workers when they see several members of a family together. For example, the parents may indicate that they have nothing to hide and invite the worker to ask whatever he wishes whilst also making it clear that certain topics are barred or that the children are not encouraged to voice their opinion. There are many reasons why social workers may have difficulty in understanding the meaning of clients' messages (Cross, 1974); sometimes these may arise for physical and psychological reasons; very often cultural factors of race, class and community will be relevant (Bernstein, 1971).

Labelling

It is sometimes tempting for social workers to label or stereotype people on the basis of the information received at the referral stage, such as the address, type of offence and age of the offender. Such information may fit into a pattern of what the worker already knows about 'people from that estate' or 'these teenage muggers'. Social workers cannot work without labels (Hardiker, 1972) but they must ensure that they go beyond the labels in their inquiry work, by individualising information in each situation (Hardiker, 1976). Though the client may also be aware that his offence and situation are not very different from those of other people around him, there is a uniqueness about the particular constellation of facts and feelings for him. For example, John Smith's probation officer knew that the family lived in temporary council accommodation and he could have had particular expectations about the sort of family he would find there and the response the offender would make to him. Instead, he ensured that he individualised this knowledge, though he set up some hypothetical points in his mind about what he might find when he visited the home. He used these as a starting point but not as a straitjacket to confirm prejudice which he might have had or that others had expressed to him about the neighbourhood.

Clients also have stereotypes about social workers and probation officers, and, this may be a further barrier to communication. For example, where social workers make inquiries on council estates that have been found to have many problems and are labelled as having many difficult residents, it is likely that many of the families will have 'anti-welfare' attitudes because their children have been removed from their care. So, before the probation officer undertakes a specific inquiry, the family may well have ideas about preventing 'the authorities' from sending someone away from home. The worker then has to show his individual and yet professional approach to the particular problem. Similarly, some middle-class people need to be encouraged to see that social workers can do more than provide unwanted material help, and can offer professional resources as carers, listeners and enablers. It is important for social workers to try to anticipate possible stereotypes which clients may have of them even if there is sometimes some justification for these clients preconceptions. Accordingly, the social worker should pitch and pace his introductions and subsequent work in inquiry situations.

The need for clarity about purpose

The importance of clarifying the purpose of the inquiry has already been stressed, otherwise there will be barriers to communication from the outset. Often, the contact in a social inquiry situation is relatively involuntary and the worker may easily feel he is intruding into the client's life. The reason for the intrusion must be established first, because workers may often be tempted to strive for acceptance and relationship. The client is much more likely to accept and relate to the social worker if he is clear about the purpose of the interview and the work they must do together. Clients and workers build up relationships through working together, even though their activities will not be very productive if relationships are not formed (Jehu, 1964). If workers are businesslike, systematic and know what they are doing, relationships will follow. Confusion over purpose may arise if a client, having been won over by the worker's efforts to reduce anxiety, sees the worker as an ally or counsel for the defence in his case.

Temptation to see change

There will be barriers to communication whenever a social worker forgets to go at the client's pace. This is an easy pitfall for social workers whose efforts are often geared to improving conditions for people or groups especially in relation to mobilising resources. When information is being collected for an inquiry, adequate knowledge has to be acquired about the client and his circumstances before planned intervention begins. Otherwise, the worker will end up pushing, directing and persuading rather than enabling and intervening on a basis of trust and confidence (McDermott, 1975).

Lack of attention

There will be barriers to communication whenever the social worker fails to pay attention to what the client is saying and indicating. This is especially likely to occur if the worker has not allowed sufficient time for his interview, and proceeds with his inquiry without ensuring sufficient privacy and freedom from interruption. It will also arise if the worker does not concentrate on what he is doing, and this often happens when he is not interested in and does not care enough about the people or because too many demands are being made upon him. Most people will be able to recall their feelings of frustration and annoyance when talking to someone who, they feel, has mentally moved to the next concern.

Recognising and dealing with normal anxiety

Most people experience some anxiety in new situations, and this will be even more apparent when strangers have to discuss a topic which in itself may be painful, embarrassing or very serious. The worker has a responsibility to bring out the normality of the anxiety whilst not being either overwhelmed by it or deflected from his purpose. John Smith's probation officer was aware of what being unemployed meant to the man and yet needed to know how, when and for what reason unemployment has arisen and continued, so that he could look at its relevance to the offence.

Cultural and social influences

Sometimes there may be seem to be resistance from the client and barriers to communication because of cultural and social differences between the worker and client. Class and cultural factors will have a bearing on what people say, the rôles they play in particular contexts and their beliefs about social work (Bernstein, 1971; Cross, 1974; Mayer and Timms, 1970). Adequate assessments cannot be made in social inquiry situations if cultural barriers to communication cannot be overcome. There is some evidence (Hardiker, 1977b) that fewer definite recommendations are made in social inquiries for immigrant offenders than in reports for white offenders. One factor in this may be cultural barriers to communication which may lead to poor assessments being made. Similarly, class perceptions about social workers will influence how much clients are willing to share. If the social worker is seen by the client as someone from the 'other side' and therefore not to be trusted, he must be aware of how he is being viewed across cultural boundaries.

Client's reluctance to find solutions because he gets gratification from his problems

The worker and client will fail to communicate in situations where the client gets satisfaction from his problems and does not want to solve them and the social worker does not perceive this. This may happen in some cases of non-attendance at school; when the social worker discusses possible ways round the problem, the parent produces another problem for each solution.

There are many reasons why communication in social inquiry situations is difficult. It is essential for the social worker to be aware of some of the sources of barriers in each situation, because he has a professional responsibility to overcome these problems in an ethical way. Whether these barriers originate in culture (class and race), structure (social inequality, criminal justice and courts) organisations (agency function and resources) or personalities, the worker has to negotiate them interpersonally in each case. There are some established principles for overcoming such barriers to communication.

Overcoming barriers to communication

Basic social work skills and processes will facilitate open and honest discussion in difficult situations.

Creating an enabling atmosphere

His skills in setting up an interview, sensitive listening and observation and sharing assessments, will help the social worker to create an appropriate climate for an inquiry interview. For example, a probation officer had to create the right climate in which to interview an adolescent offender under his supervision. He described how he did this:

> I specifically went and asked him to come in and talk about
> this offence because I had to write a report for the court. That
> interview gave an indication of the constraints I felt about
> communication with this boy, in that the interview took place
> in our group room half over a game of table tennis. It was on
> that sort of level—a very shallow interview which basically was
> fact-finding on my part and not really much to do with feelings.
> It was in that interview that he mentioned that the boy whom

he hit said something about him not having a father, which I thought was a fairly crucial piece of information. That was an unexpected pay off, because I was just asking him where he was standing, what were his injuries, etc. . .

Limiting and facilitating information

Some clients are willing to share too much for the purpose of the inquiry, whilst others are unable to share anything; either way, these are barriers to communication which need to be overcome. Sometimes, for example, it may be particularly difficult to limit what parents wish to convey when an adolescent is the main client. If there has been previous tension with the youngster, the parent is often glad of the opportunity to discuss the problem. If at the same time the family is undergoing some other crisis and they are given the chance to talk, it is difficult to limit them to focus on the current inquiry. Discussions between worker and client may then become loosely structured and sometimes the worker must have the patience and skill to listen and distinguish between what he needs for current purposes and what may be 'left on ice' until another time.

A social worker in any social inquiry situation walks a metaphorical tightrope, needing to ask questions but not doing so either in a way which leaves no room for the client to comment, or by engaging in aimless talk. If a client feels he has been allowed to tell only half of his story, he will find it hard to believe the worker when he says, 'yes, I see what you mean'. Conversely, the person who has launched into his story and cannot stop, may need containing so that he does not feel he has exposed more of himself in an interview than he intended. The worker has a responsibility to enable, encourage and help a client to express his thoughts and feelings about the topic of the inquiry as far as he comfortably can.

Confidentiality

This is a central aspect of all social work, and is particularly crucial when information is being collected for an inquiry report which will be presented in a public court. The worker must share with the client the nature and purpose of any confidential matter which may be used; otherwise the client will—quite rightly—feel betrayed and misunderstood. Another side of confidentiality is that clients should be asked if the worker may interview another person. It is then no surprise to the client when information gleaned is discussed. Respecting basic social work principles such as confidentiality will be yet another means of overcoming barriers to communication.

The worker's own personality

Though social workers bring their skills, knowledge and values to social inquiry situations, an important factor on which they rely for communication with their clients is their own personalities. The social worker needs to feel the security obtained through proper preparation for the task he undertakes. He has to be able to stand up to stress and criticism and, whilst showing he is not destroyed by it, he must also show that he is sensitive to feeling. He has to withstand pressure sometimes to let a point go rather than pursue it and yet if he loses hold of that point he may not reach it again with the client. Consequently, collusion and superficiality follows in their work together.

There are many ways in which social workers can overcome barriers to communication in social inquiry situations: creating an enabling atmosphere, facilitating and limiting information, using his own personality and remembering his basic social work principles of confidentiality, self-determination, acceptance and respect for the client. There are skills in creating the right balance between protecting and enabling clients to share what they feel able to about the subject of the inquiry. After all, profound issues are at stake in many inquiry situations and the worker has a professional responsibility to communicate openly and responsibly with the relevant people.

We have referred to the case of John Smith on several occasions in this chapter because there were indications that the points we were making about the acquisition of information were demonstrated in that inquiry. The probation officer went to a number of sources for information but used the interviews with the man and his wife as the main basis for the information he wished to convey to the court. He discussed with the client information he collected, and considered how that differed from the client's view of events. As he went into the first interview, he had certain hypotheses in mind which began to form the framework for seeking the information he knew he required for the court. As he acquired some of the facts and feelings of the situation, he checked and reviewed what he was told. For example, because one aspect of the man's unemployment was related to health factors, the family doctor's opinion was sought in confirmation. Because the family's financial position was made more difficult by the payment of rent arrears as well as current expenses, he checked out with the housing department how these had to be met. The worker knew, from observation and contact with the family, some of the strengths and some of the problems that were present but, because of the boundaries of his function at the inquiry stage, he did not begin to contract with the client how these might be tackled. The worker selected from the information he acquired the 'reliable, relevant and comprehensive' data which he saw as helpful for the court to make an 'appropriate' decision.

Practice theories in the acquisition of information

As social workers acquire the first facts about a new referral, they begin to make choices about their significance and to link such information with their own thoughts, feelings and observations about a case. The filtering process, by which many sources of knowledge are used and some sense is made of a complex situation, starts at the outset of any inquiry, it sets the scene for the kind of information sought, the methods used to collect it and the sense to be made of it. Practice theories refer to the process of using and integrating professional experience and knowledge in a skilful and ethical manner.

In the case of John Smith, the probation officer drew on some explicit theories of practice as he filtered the information he acquired. The fact of a disrupted childhood assumed significance. The themes of insecurity, inadequacy and rejection in the client's life seemed relevant because of his current deteriorating employment, his financial problems, poor health and the complexity of his environmental circumstances. These theories of practice were drawn from an explicitly psycho-dynamic base, interwoven with the belief that other systems in the client's social environment were also relevant. Even so, the worker had to rely on other evidence, such as his observations about Mr Smith and his family within the context of their home and his feelings about Mr Smith's responsibilities for his own actions. Perhaps the practice theories which brought all these thoughts, feelings and observations together were based on a psycho-social idea about the way in which some people try to solve their life problems.

Chapter three

Skills and methods in studying facts and feelings

We argued in the previous chapter that probation officers should not merely collect a list of facts when they are making assessments—they must be sensitive to what is involved in the process of gathering information. Next they must study the situation, trying to fit together facts and feelings about it, and finding some orderly pattern in the case. One of the ways in which they do this is by giving priority to some factors over others. For example, probation officers collect information about some facts more frequently and consistently than others (Hardiker, 1975). They almost always give priority to the following: the offence and circumstances, the previous criminal record, the offender's family and personality. This indicates that probation officers keep firmly in mind one of the reasons why they are involved in a case—their client is charged with criminal offences and may have previous convictions. They also work firmly with the client's immediate situation—either his own needs, feelings and attitudes, or his family circumstances. This stress on the 'reality' factor of the offence(s) and the immediate personal and social situation of the offender is one way in which probation officers can begin to study the situation with which they are working.

It also illustrates quite clearly that social work is not about either the 'individual' or the 'society' in isolation from one another, but is concerned with the person-society connection—that is, relationships between people in groups. The specific role of the social worker in these circumstances is to identify the problems people may encounter in their relationships, and situations; for example, stealing to buy food because they are poor, or assaulting a child or spouse in response to family tensions. His task is also to identify the problem-solving capacities of a person in relation to his crime, his situation, and his own needs and strengths.

As social work shifts its model from a relatively individualistic to an interactionist or social system framework for studying cases and conceptualising practice theory, it could be argued that the probation officers whose work we describe were adopting an outmoded paradigm in concentrating on the crime and the offender. This is a problem which will be examined in greater detail in the last chapter. For the moment we shall describe some of the ways in which probation officers handle the material which they gather about their clients.

The relevance of frameworks

We saw above that probation officers need to be sensitive about the process of collecting their information and that they must have some framework of relevance for the facts they gather. Why is it important to know about the offence—the police already have details? Why is it necessary to assess the offender's personal and social circumstances? What bearing does (or should) the sentencing policy of the court have on their deliberations? It seems that probation officers have very specific reasons for studying particular factors, such as offence, family and social circumstances and court policies. The reasons they give for considering them illustrate a very complex process of studying and fitting together a variety of data in their social inquiry work. For example, they think of offences either in terms of their relative seriousness or as a 'cry for help'; the offender's circumstances are seen as either a source of support or sign of stress; the sentencing policy of the court is something to be either accepted or negotiated.

Offence factors

The offence(s) and previous criminal record are always relevant factors in social inquiry assessments, and there are a variety of ways in which they may be studied.

The offence and circumstances

Probation officers typically gather information about the circumstances of the offence in order to come to some conclusion about either its seriousness or its meaning.

(a) Sometimes it is concluded that the offence is relatively trivial; for example, an adolescent boy was charged with theft of cakes following a street prank. The probation officer suggested to the court that as, 'he was not involved in the initial phase of the incident and was to some extent a victim of circumstances', a conditional discharge would be suitable.

(b) At other times, it emerges that the offences are relatively serious and probation officers have to acknowledge this; for example, a youth was jointly charged with two offences of theft as trespasser involving goods valued at several hundred pounds. The probation officer concluded that the offence was serious, not only because of the value of the goods, but also because he, 'thought it out, planned it, decided that this was what he wanted, weighed up the risks and went and did it'; a detention centre was recommended.

(c) On the other hand, whether the offence is officially serious or trivial, the probation officer might conclude that it is a 'cry for help'. For example, a married couple were charged with theft of food valued at about one pound, and the probation officer thought that the offence was a 'cry for help' because the whole episode revolved around their current family circumstances: the wife had psychiatric problems, there were marital and financial difficulties, and if the offence had not been committed, their problems would probably have come out in another way, such as a suicide attempt. In another case, a man was charged with theft involving several hundred pounds (he had embezzled on his laundry round), and the probation officer thought that the offence was a 'cry for help', by an 'insecure, immature and isolated' man who had many personal and family problems. Probation was recommended in both these cases because the probation officers studied the offences in relation to the offenders' individualised needs rather than the tariff.

Previous criminal record

Social workers usually consider their clients in relation to both their current situation and their previous life experiences. In its more extreme form, psychiatric social histories include accounts of the very early developmental experience of clients. Even though probation officers rarely consider an offender's early history in just this way, they do not ignore their client's background, especially their previous criminal history.

(a) Some offenders are appearing in court for the first time (and it is officially recommended that social inquiry reports should be prepared on all adult first offenders—Home Office Circular 188/68); for example, a man was jointly charged with burglary and had no previous convictions. The fact that it was his first offence was one of the things the probation officer took into account in recommending a financial penalty to the court.

(b) Sometimes an offender's previous criminal record appears to be so serious that the probation officer acknowledges this in his assessment; for example, an eighteen-year-old man was jointly charged with six offences of theft and deception, and had five previous court appearances; the probation officer acknowledged the inevitability of a custodial sentence, commenting,

I think in any court (the judicial system being what it is), if a young man comes up with as many offences against him past and present, it is fairly inevitable he is going to get a prison sentence.

(c) There is another way, however, in which the probation officer considers the relevance of a serious criminal record; it may be seen as an indication that the offender is pushed into repeated crimes by circumstances beyond his control. For example, a young man was charged with several motoring offences and had a long criminal record; the probation officer considered that his current offence was similar in pattern to his previous ones, and whilst he 'could not discount his record, the fact that he had done it so many times made it more serious because it displayed an almost compulsive need to be caught because he was sort of committing suicide'. So a current offence in relation to a serious criminal record may be seen in terms of the offender's personality—a 'compulsive need to be caught' or a 'cry for help'.

Accordingly, the offence and criminal record may be studied in a variety of ways. Their relative seriousness may be given priority or it may be felt that they are related to an offender's underlying problems and thus a 'cry for help'. Crimes are referral issues for probation officers, and great skill is needed in identifying their relevance for individual offenders and agency function. Part of the skill lies in conveying to offenders the significance of the offence and previous criminal record.

Offender factors

Offenders are people in social groups—families, communities, schools and work-places. As such they may meet ordinary problems, they have adequate coping-mechanisms and sufficient supports to help with stresses in their environment. Alternatively their problem-solving capacities may indicate that they are in 'need' of help. Probation officers appear to operate on the basis of these assumptions when they are studying offenders.

The offender's family

Probation officers frequently consider the offender in relation to his family, and this is especially so in the case of juveniles.

   (a) Sometimes, the offender's family is seen to present no problems and to offer support to him. For example, a youth was charged with drinking under age, and the probation officer thought that intervention was not necessary because he had, 'warm and caring parents who offered him sensible advice', and he recommended a financial penalty accordingly.

   (b) Alternatively, an offender's family may be seen as the source of his problems; for example a thirteen-year-old boy was charged with theft as trespasser and had no previous convictions; the probation officer thought that his offence behaviour was partly associated with problems in his family, as he explained:

I think it is a marital problem, not unrelated to cultural difficulties; his family came to England in the hope of improving their circumstances and perhaps found it more of a struggle than they expected and in that sense frustrations have not helped the marital relationship. Father has tended to seek a bit of escape in drink at times. Mother has had to go out to work and has begun to try and achieve a certain amount of independence from the husband, which does not fit in with his expectations. I think this has some direct bearing on the boy's behaviour because the family situation is one in which conflict is quite apparent; it does not help him feel secure in his family and again he has this problem of finding out his own identity. The parents have unrealistic ambitions for their children. Therefore, he committed this offence along with his mates for reasons of status and group membership.

In these cases, the probation officers are studying the offender within the context of his family; sometimes they find no problems and feel that the parents are offering sufficient support; in other cases, the offences appear to be related to specific problems in the family which is considered to be a suitable focus for social work intervention.

The offender's personality

Probation officers consider the offender's personality more frequently than any other factor in the course of their social inquiry work.

(a) Sometimes, the offender has few personal problems; for example an adolescent was charged with theft, and the probation officer thought that he was a stable, well-adjusted boy who did not need supervision, so a conditional discharge was recommended.

(b) In contrast, the offender's personality might be seen as the focus of his problems; for example a thirteen-year-old boy was charged with breaking and entering and the probation officer thought that this was tied up with the fact that he was in the midst of adolescent changes, and 'being a verbally inexpressive person might be unknowingly seeking to express himself in actions which are as perplexing for him as they are for his family'.

So the offender's personal strengths or areas of need seem to be significant factors which probation officers study when they are trying to make sense of the situation they are assessing.

The neighbourhood and community context of the offender

Probation officers do not confine themselves to the immediate context of offenders, because they also consider the wider situation in which they live, such as housing, neighbours and community.

(a) In some cases, the community in which an offender lives is seen to be providing him with adequate support. For example, a twenty-one-year-old man from Asia was charged with obtaining money by deception, and one of the factors which led the probation officer to conclude that he did not need social work supervision was that he was a member of the local African-Asian community which was serving as support for him.

(b) Just as a community can be a support for an offender, it might also be a source of pressure; for example, a seventeen-year-old youth was charged with theft, and his criminal career was thought to be tied up with his general environment and neighbourhood where he lived—'these were the pressures with which he was having to contend—he lives on a well-known "problem estate" where there are a lot of young people amongst whom it is more acceptable to break the law than to uphold it given the opportunity to do either'. This will often be a difficult aspect for the probation officer to discuss with the offender; he should show understanding and readiness to consider such community pressures, even if he does not condone them.

The community in which offenders live seems to be a very important consideration when probation officers are studying the source of their clients' problems and deciding on the supports and resources available to them if they need help. Some offences may be seen as relatively 'normal', given the community norms of the people committing them.

The economic circumstances of the offender

Some offenders seem to have few financial problems whilst others appear to be in dire financial straits; these factors need to be considered because they might be a source of the offender's problems or they may indicate some of the ways in which he may be helped. For example:

(a) A youth was charged with theft of lead and copper wire; one of the factors taken into account when it was decided to recommend a fine was that he was in full employment and had no great financial claims on him.

(b) One offender's financial problems on the other hand appeared to be seen as a symptom of his underlying difficulties. As we have already seen, in one case the probation officer described how his client,

runs up debts and complains about them but has made no effort in the past to pay them off; he lives in temporary council accommodation where he has several items of material things which perhaps other families would not have bought until they paid off their rent arrears.

(c) Sometimes an offender's financial poverty is taken into account in recommending a particular sentence. For example, a conditional discharge was recommended for a woman charged with assault following a domestic quarrel. The probation officer gave her reasons in the court report as follows:

Mrs Bates does not work and at the time of preparation of this report Mr Bates has been dismissed from his job following a series of apparently unavoidable absences. To date he has made no social security claim and is hopeful of obtaining work soon. It would therefore appear that Mrs Bates is not in a position to meet any financial penalty.

Therefore, an offender's economic circumstances may be studied in terms of the appropriateness of a financial penalty, or poverty may be thought to be a symptom of the offender's problems. Usually, economic factors are so linked with social and personal circumstances that it is difficult to study their significance with the client at this stage of the assessment process.

Social factors

Most offenders have friends and go to either school or work, and these factors might be studied in a social inquiry assessment.

(a) Sometimes an offender's social situation is seen to be supportive; for example, an adolescent was doing well at school and had lots of hobbies so he was not seen to be in need of social work assistance and a conditional discharge was recommended.

(b) Just as social factors may be a source of support, they might also be an indication of need; for example, one offender's problems were thought to be connected with work, 'because he was beginning to lose confidence in himself and was almost afraid to go out and go to work'; the probation officer found him a job he liked and it seemed to be working out quite well; so in this case, a suspended sentence supervision order was recommended to the court.

Health factors

The mental and physical health of an offender and others close to him is always an important area to study in a social inquiry.

(a) Sometimes, the probation officer may be confident after relevant questioning that health is not an area of need or related to the referral problem, and may not need to say anything in his report about this issue.

(b) But if there has been a significant illness this may be very relevant in the social inquiry. For example, in one case a married woman was charged with a shop-lifting offence and the probation officer related the whole episode to her health situation, commenting,

> I did not think she was fully aware of what was going on because of her ill-health. She had just had a hysterectomy, had nervous trouble and was walking about the store 'in a daze'. The offence was very much related to her health.

We have tried to show in these examples then that probation officers consider many factors in a variety of ways when they are studying clients' situations. Sometimes they concentrate on the relative seriousness of the offence or alternatively see it as a 'cry for help' related to the offender's background. A variety of factors in the offender's life may be taken into account, such as his family, his personal attitudes, his community and his economic, health and social circumstances. These may be seen either to indicate no problems and to offer support, or they may appear to be the source of the offender's problems and an area which indicates the need for social work intervention. It is important for probation officers to share their assessments of the various factors they study at this stage; what may seem to the probation officer to be a stress to the client may not actually be experienced as such by the offender, or the latter may be experiencing problems from areas which may appear to be a source of support, such as his family.

These illustrations suggest that probation officers operate midway between a justice model which lays stress on the offence alone, and a psycho-dynamic model in which a person's psyche *may* be analysed separately from his criminality and his wider social context. This is what the neo-classical revisions to criminal justice were all about (Taylor, Walton and Young, 1973), because they allowed some individual differences between offenders to be taken into account, either in mitigation of sentence or as a pointer to a rehabilitative sentence. For example, the age, mental condition and previous criminal record of an offender may indicate that he has less free will than most adult (rational) men; such people should therefore receive a lesser punishment or be recommended for a treatment measure such as probation. The personal and social circumstances of an offender may be taken into account in a similar manner (Hardiker and Webb, 1978).

Social control factors

So far we have described some of the ways in which probation officers study information about offenders and their offences. However, their own professional and work situation is an equally important area for them to study, and they need to consider the sentencing policy of the court and the policies and function of their own agency.

Sentencing policy of the courts

This is a factor which is frequently taken into account by probation officers, and it is important for social workers to remember why and for whom they are preparing social inquiries. In the case of probation officers the information they collect and study must be relevant to the court (The Streatfeild Report, 1961).

(a) *Legitimation* Social workers cannot help everyone in need, probation officers are subject to the rule of law and must give some consideration to an offender's criminal behaviour. This is both a boundary and an opportunity in their social inquiry work. The probation officer is legitimated to 'enquire in accordance with any direction of the court' (Powers of Criminal Courts Act, 1973) into the circumstances of only particular people—those in the dock. What kind of assistance sentencers request or receive remains a critical issue, but probation officers often seem to keep in mind an offender's criminal behaviour (Hardiker, 1975). Sometimes, they refer to this explicitly in their social inquiry reports, by either offering a diagnosis for someone's criminal behaviour or suggesting a prognosis for his reform and a sentence which might 'curb his criminal tendencies' (Hardiker, 1978). At other times, probation officers see the social inquiry as an opportunity for helping an offender and his family with some personal problem. This is most clearly seen in those cases when they think the offence is a 'cry for help' or a 'pointer to the need for social work intervention'. The legitimation of social work should be a potential safeguard against violations of due process in the courts. Nevertheless, this remains a profound problem for social work in the courts, but it cannot be elaborated further here.

(b) *Suitability for probation*   Another way in which the sentencing policy of the court might be studied is by assessing an offender's suitability for probation. Haines (1975) points out that clients must be assessed as belonging to a particular category defined by law or agency procedure, though Sainsbury (1970) reminds us that agency function is not necessarily something the worker passively accepts. At its simplest, no one can be put on probation, fined or sent to prison unless he has been found guilty of a criminal act; usually, an offender's appearance in court will legitimate the probation officer's social inquiry. But suitability for probation is also assessed in terms of agency policy and resources. For example, the workers in a probation intake team recommended fewer offenders for probation than their colleagues in another agency (see Hardiker, 1977b). Furthermore, an offender must be 'willing' to meet the conditions of a probation order, and some people on whom reports are prepared request a classical justice sentence rather than probation. Sometimes offenders are not thought to be 'suitable' for probation. This takes us back to a central feature of all social work—clients should preferably display motivation and capacity for change if help is to be offered. Suitability for probation is a more complex topic, but it is relevant to all social inquiry work. It is sometimes argued (The Morison Report, 1962) that this should be given primacy in any recommendation.

(c) *Anticipating the sentencers*   The sentencing policy of the court will also set a framework for the probation officer's thinking, and this happens when the likely response of the bench to a case is anticipated. For example, it is sometimes accepted that a custodial sentence is inevitable, given the seriousness of an offender's criminal record; in other cases a financial penalty seems to be a foregone conclusion. These are factors probation officers must always study, whether or not in the end they decide to bow to the inevitable sentence or actively attempt to influence the court's decision. And they can only do this if they 'know their court'.

The policy, resources and functions of the probation agency

These must be a context for social inquiry studies in two respects: they set boundaries to the actual social inquiry assessment and they provide guidelines for the kinds of help available within the agency.

(a) *Agency policy and function*   First, different probation departments may have different policies in respect of pre-trial and remand inquiries. Some agencies prepare predominantly pre-trial reports on either all offenders before the court or particular categories of offenders, whilst other agencies undertake primarily remand reports. This will be an important consideration for the probation officer. If the tradition is to prepare pre-trial reports, some social inquiries will be conducted in situations in which an offender is pleading not guilty. Consequently, the offender may be very sensitive to the social inquiry, so relevant factors must be studied whilst his rights are simultaneously respected. In these circumstances, it may also be very difficult to study the offender's needs in isolation from his possible criminal activities which cannot be investigated if there is a 'not guilty' plea. The preparation of social inquiry reports in 'not guilty' cases has always been a critical issue in the probation service (see Plotnikoff, 1973). It has taken on a new urgency, since the National Association of Probation Officers has recommended that reports should not be prepared in these cases.

There are many variations between probation agencies in this respect and it is important for social workers to learn the policies and procedures of their own areas in these cases.

Second, probation agencies will have policies about which cases they can help and which must be passed on to other departments. For example, an elderly man with a long criminal record appeared before the court on a trivial charge. He had many marital, health and financial problems but the probation officer thought that he needed home-help and social services support rather than probation supervision and recommended a conditional discharge.

(b) *Agency resources*   Factors such as manpower and size of caseload must also be considered in social inquiries; these will influence which offenders will have pre-trial reports prepared on them and whether there are resources available for various kinds of probation supervision. For example, in one agency pre-trial reports were prepared on all offenders appearing before the courts at one stage, but gradually the agency had to refine its criteria because the demand for reports could not be met. In other circumstances, caseloads may be so high that few offenders are recommended for probation (Hardiker, 1975, 1977b). Probation officers must be very clear about their professional responsibilities when faced with such pressures of work, because they raise profound implications for their social inquiry work. For example, an offender's 'needs' may be 'played down' in a report in order to support a recommendation for a conditional discharge rather than a probation order (*ibid.*).

Whether he accepts them or fights them, the policy, function and resources in the agency are important areas for the probation officer to study in his social inquiry work.

Probation officer styles

Questions about policy, resources and function are never clear-cut, of course, but they always set a framework for the probation officer's study. Most of all, the probation officer must be clear that a social inquiry report is a sentencing document and not a casework assessment. If he is clear about these boundaries, then it is perfectly appropriate for him to be flexible about some of the factors he negotiates during his study. For example, sometimes, the triviality of a juvenile offence will not warrant supervision but the needs of the parents might indicate the appropriateness of this; parents may completely over-react or fail to cope with a delinquent episode and the probation officer must study very carefully whether a supervision order would be an appropriate means of helping the parents (with all the due process and justice issues this raises) by, for example, building up their confidence about their parental functions. This must be studied alongside the other possibility that such supervision might undermine rather than build up the parents' confidence.

A trickier issue—rarely acknowledged—is that sometimes probation officers study social situations from a very personal point of view. For example, a woman was charged with theft and the probation officer considered recommending probation, but said,

> I rejected supervision because she was leaving the area and she
> would not have seen the need for it. And quite a big factor,
> was that I had to grapple with my own strong feelings of dislike
> for this woman; I knew the court would fine her if supervision
> was not suggested.

This is a negative form of discrimination, but it may operate for more positive reasons too. For example, there may be cases in which the worker's rather than the offender's needs colour the study and lead to a recommendation for probation when there are few indications that this is needed. This may arise because the probation officer has an affinity with particular types of personality (for example, anti-authority) or particular interests in family therapy. The family's needs may not justify probation but the officer sees potential for a better functioning family group if some work is done to remove communication blocks. Such areas of discretion are rarely explicitly acknowledged though they are increasingly being recognised as problems for analysis in social work (Parsloe, 1976). Whether the reasons are relatively positive or negative, there are pressures here for very unprofessional and undemocratic work to be done. The ethics of service, the legitimation and sentencing policy of the court, the function, policies and resources of the agency and the probation officer's own professionalism should together ensure that the offender's needs and rights are protected and met. One step in this direction may be to make such processes more explicit.

We have tried to show then in this section that when the probation officer is studying facts and feelings, he is not doing so as a kind of free-floating observer. His study is contextualised, and he must consider the sentencing policy of the court, the policy, function and resources of his own agency, his own biases and preferences, and other agencies and supports which may be available. We have illustrated some of the ways in which any one of these contexts may bias the picture he sees and the sense he makes of it. Once again, it is important that the probation officer shares his study of social control factors with the offender, so that the latter understands that sometimes the sentencing policy of the court and the function of the agency have to be accepted, whereas in other situations some negotiations may take place.

Frameworks for study

It has been necessary for purposes of description and analysis to present the factors probation officers study in relatively discrete sections: offence, offender and social control. However, this gives an artificial and oversimplified picture of the actual processes of study.

First, probation officers study cases from the perspective of particular theories and frameworks. As we saw in the first chapter, Mr Smith's probation officer approached that particular case from a mainly psycho-dynamic perspective, which meant that the theft offences were interpreted as a symptom of the offender's feelings of rejection and inadequacy. Other probation officers employ a more sociological approach in their social inquiry studies, and think of offence behaviour in terms of drift, opportunity, risk and delinquent subcultures rather than psychopathology. Different probation officers may, therefore, study their social inquiries from contrasting theoretical perspectives.

Second, even if different probation officers approach their social inquiries from different theoretical perspectives, this does not necessarily mean that there are inconsistencies between them as they study their cases. This is a complex topic which has been elaborated on elsewhere (Hardiker 1977a, Hardiker and Webb 1978), and the concept of ideology is one means of exploring it. Briefly, ideologies refer to relatively abstract bodies of ideas, beliefs and interests which are systematic enough to portray an underlying attitude amongst the members of the social group who adhere to them. For example, politicians, professionals and administrators may hold distinctive occupational ideologies. Ideologies are difficult to identify because they tend to be relatively implicit. Even so, there is some evidence (*ibid*.) that probation officers use treatment ideologies in some of their social inquiries, which means that they relate offence behaviour to an offender's personal and social problems and think in terms of the need for social work intervention. Interestingly, but not surprisingly since they are in a helping profession, most probation officers—whether they are psycho-dynamically or sociologically oriented—hold such a treatment ideology towards some of their cases. 'Need' may be located in either an offender's psychopathology or social situation; either way, social work intervention may be considered appropriate.

Thirdly, some evidence (*ibid*.) suggests that the circumstances of the case being studied have a bearing on the kind of ideology held towards it. If a probation officer holds a treatment ideology in a social inquiry (that is, he interprets the offences in terms of the offender's problems), it is likely that the offence(s) will be relatively serious and that the offender will be experiencing a variety of personal, material and social stresses in his life. There seem to be more similarities than differences between probation officers in the ways they study their social inquiry cases and every probation officer will be treatment-oriented towards some of his cases. Most probation officers will hold treatment ideologies in some of their cases and non-treatment ideologies in others. We shall illustrate this by examining another piece of work completed by John Smith's probation officer.

As we saw in Chapter one, the probation officer studied John Smith's situation within a treatment-ideology framework. The theft offences were thought to be related to Mr Smith's financial problems, but the probation officer also felt that there were more complex underlying reasons for them, including Smith's loss of masculine pride. The probation officer thought that the offences were a symptom of Smith's underlying personal problems and a pointer to the need for social work intervention. It was not seen to be a case in which the offences were a calculated risk unrelated to Smith's previous and current personal situation.

John Smith's probation officer approached another social inquiry within a rather different framework; even though he still asked some psycho-dynamic questions in the case, he concluded his study with a non-treatment ideology. Tim Jones, aged twenty-one, was charged in the crown court with allowing his premises to be used for smoking cannabis. He lived in a bed-sitting room in a large dwelling house, and as he had a hi-fi system, other young people used his room communally. Cannabis-smoking was introduced as part of their fellowship together and the flat was raided by the police.

First, Tim Jones was aware that cannabis-smoking was an offence but he had philosophical reasons for continuing to smoke. The probation officer was in sympathy with Tim Jones, agreed with him that cannabis-smoking with consent was not as harmful as people tried to make out that it was, and felt that a young man aged twenty-one ought to be able to make up his own mind about it.

Second, the probation officer thought that Tim Jones was reasonably well-adjusted, commenting, 'I saw him as a confident, intelligent person, and someone who not only enjoyed his life but had definite reasons why he should enjoy his life and could also articulate those reasons.'

There were various question marks about Tim Jones's situation. Whilst Tim's family relationships appeared stable, his mother struck the probation officer as 'a very irritable, fussy kind of person who worried tremendously about Tim'. Furthermore, Tim was in financial debt and had been dismissed from a previous job for poor time-keeping. He was currently working as a security officer, but had been on two trips abroad 'to travel and see the world and to gain some experience of Eastern religions, beliefs and practice.' The probation officer was uncertain as to whether Tim Jones's trips were motivated by a genuine desire to see the world, an attempt to live an imaginative life, or whether they were a symptom of his inability to settle down. On balance he felt that it was less to do with personal malfunctioning and more to do with a genuine desire to see the world.

Third, Tim Jones's probation officer considered recommending a probation order, which would have given him a chance, 'to monitor what was happening a bit more and then decide later on whether Tim needed more treatment, or whether the original recommendation for a fine had been the right one'. In the end he decided to recommend a fine, because Tim Jones was obviously determined to set off on his world travels again: 'On balance I thought a fine was appropriate because it was Tim Jones's first offence, and if he offended again there would be some kind of pattern that would have emerged by then.' The court fined Tim Jones £60; and whilst the probation officer had expected the maximum fine, he hoped it might be less, given the mitigating circumstances he presented in the social inquiry report.

It may seem surprising that it was the same probation officer who studied both John Smith and Tim Jones. Smith's theft offences were thought to be related to financial pressures and loss of masculine pride, whilst Jones's philosophical explanations for his drug offences were accepted at face value. The variety of personal and social stresses in Smith's background were seen to be contributory factors towards the offence behaviour, whereas the pressures in Jones's life were cancelled out as relevant to the offence. The probation officer's psycho-dynamic orientation led him to ask questions about the meaning of the offence in relation to the offender's personality in each case, but it produced two very different sets of answers respectively. The probation officer concluded his study of John Smith's case with a treatment ideology, which meant that the theft offences were seen to be related to the offender's personal and social problems for which social work intervention through a probation order seemed appropriate. In contrast, he concluded his study of Tim Jones's case with a non-treatment ideology, because he thought the drug offences were not related to the offender's possible problems and decided that they were not a pointer to the need for social work intervention. (The reader may think that the comparison between a theft and a cannabis offence is unfair and inappropriate, but another comparable case could have been presented in which John Smith's probation officer employed a non-treatment ideology in the case of a woman charged with theft.)

It is difficult to identify why the probation officer held contrasting ideologies in these two cases. It could be that the probation officer understood and sympathised with Jones's philosophical explanations for his offences, whereas it was less easy for him to accept political explanations for Smith's theft offences, even if these were well articulated by the offender. Because the probation officer could identify himself with Jones's drug offences, he might have found it easier to 'put himself in the offender's shoes' and accept that he was self-determining. This probably held him back from exploring the mother/son relationship further, which his psychodynamic orientation would normally lead him to do. The probation officer was engaged in a complex filtering process as he studied Tim Jones and, as he admitted, he found the case a challenge to him.

As we pointed out in the first chapter, it is the process of using different kinds of knowledge in social work which we need to try to understand; even if the probation officer came to very different conclusions in these two cases, he filtered a mass of data and made some sense of the situation by studying the offenders' respective offences in the contexts of their rather different personal/social situations. Perhaps psycho-dynamic explanations fitted Smith's case rather neatly, whereas the probation officer resorted to his own personal beliefs in order to handle the Jones inquiry. The offenders were similar in age, but the probation officer probably felt an affinity for Jones which he did not feel for Smith. Smith was probably also more typical of the type of people handled in the probation agency and therefore, familiar to the probation officer; it might have been more difficult to think of appropriate ways of working with Jones in a probation order. It is impossible for anyone to know what swung the balance in these two cases; it seems likely that the probation officer was engaged in a complex filtering process as he made his assessment, and that he would have to rely on his own feelings, hunches and observations in addition to any social work or social science theories which were available to him.

Whenever social workers study facts and feelings, they do this within the context of a professional relationship in an agency setting. The referral issue provides a focus for study, and the disposals and interventions available will also be anticipated as the social worker tries to make sense of the case before him and shares his assessment with the offender. As he is studying his data, the social worker will usually have one eye on the need to formulate an assessment and come to some recommendation or conclusion in his social inquiry report. For example, as he begins to identify areas and sources of problems in an offender's life (family, community, work) he will start thinking about possible targets and methods of intervention. If there are marital or psychiatric problems, he must consider the resources available for such help in that area. On the other hand, the offender may seem to have so many problems that he and others are at risk if he stays in the community. The needs of the offender may be suitable for help through a probation order. This shows once again that the stages in any assessment are inextricably linked and that the assessment process in social inquiries involves much more than an *ad hoc* colllection of facts.

Knowledge about social workers' ideologies is still very limited (Hardiker, 1977a, Parsloe, 1976; Smith and Harris, 1972; Smith, 1977), but it is likely that ideologies will constitute an important element in practice theories. Treatment ideologies about crime may be one means by which probation officers can make sense of and filter a mass of data about some offenders on whom social inquiries are prepared. The ideas and beliefs underlying such ideologies may be relatively implicit and not based exclusively on social science knowledge. This is why ideologies are more likely to be practice theories rather than theories of practice.

Chapter four

Skills and methods in formulating an assessment

Haines (1975, p. 42) describes the process of formulating an assessment as a weighing process in which positive and negative factors are balanced. As we have seen in previous chapters, this process will start at the very beginning of any assessment. For example, the relative seriousness of the offence will be studied alongside strengths and stresses in an offender's life, and these will be considered in the context of the sentencing policy of the court and the probation officer's agency function. We have also seen that offence, offender and social control factors are rarely considered in isolation from one another during social inquiry assessments. For example, the criminal activities of an offender are considered in relation to his personal and social situation rather than as isolated offences which have no meaning to the person—how else could it be concluded that sometimes an offence appears to be a 'cry for help'! Furthermore, such considerations will usually be made with a view to a future outcome—a sentence in court.

We shall now describe the formulation stage as a rather more systematic process in which the probation officer sums up his assessment in the form of a balance sheet. The equation he makes usually includes a consideration of risk, need and resources. Sometimes, the *risk* of an offender committing more crimes is seen to be so great that a custodial sentence is acknowledged to protect either the offender or the community. In other cases, an offender's *needs* seem to be so great that nothing else but probation is considered. In other situations, the availability of *resources* seems to influence the decision. Usually, however, risk, need and resources have to be weighed up one against the other and the probation officer must be willing actively to negotiate the assessment he has formulated with the court.

Risk

At the formulation stage, the probation officer may conclude that the risk of an offender committing further offences is either minimal, moderate or great; his recommendation may reflect this accordingly.

Conditional discharge

An adolescent boy was charged with theft following a street prank. Summing up the nature of his offence, previous record, circumstances and the sentencing policy of the court, the probation officer decided that he was not at risk because he had no previous convictions and was a victim of circumstances in the crime.

Fine

A young man was charged with abstracting electricity. The probation officer weighed up whether to recommend a conditional discharge or fine, and decided that the court would not see a conditional discharge as punitive enough, that a suspended sentence was not merited on grounds of risk, and a fine was recommended.

Probation

An adolescent girl was charged with theft from a store. The probation officer weighed up the seriousness of the offences which had been committed over a period of time, the underlying difficulties in family relationships, and concluded that supervision was appropriate, especially since, 'her parents were not saying she was out of control so a care order was not called for'. Supervision seemed appropriate given the degree of risk.

A young man was charged with several serious driving offences and had a long record. The probation officer thought he needed help and treatment more than anything else; he acknowledged that the court would see the case as very serious because, 'there were three lots of offences, one after the other and I was pretty certain that the court would have to be punitive and send him to prison because they would see him as a menace to society and dangerous'. However, he recommended probation as an alternative to imprisonment because he was prepared to continue helping him.

Custody

Sometimes, the risk of further offences is so great that the inevitability of a custodial sentence is acknowledged. For example, a young man was charged with several offences of deception and joint conspiracy to steal, and had numerous previous convictions. He had committed further offences whilst on bail and the probation officer summed up his formulation as follows:

> The offences prevented me thinking of anything other than a custodial sentence. His previous criminal record obviously ties in with that. In bowing to the inevitability of a custodial sentence, I was feeling that his personality did not need outside social work intervention. On balance the next stage is a prison sentence, given the sentencing policy of the court and the fact that open treatment had not been successful.

It seems then from these examples that probation officers formulate their assessments in terms of a crude tariff relating to risk. If this is minimal, a conditional discharge or fine may be recommended; if it is moderate, a probation order may be suggested; when there is maximum risk, the inevitability of a custodial sentence may be acknowledged.

Need

If offenders have personal or social difficulties, this may be taken as an indication of need in a social inquiry assessment.

Conditional discharge

There are two different ways in which an assessment may be formulated on the basis of need. First, as we saw in the previous chapter, the offence in some cases seems to be either trivial or rational and the offender does not appear to be under any personal or social stresses. In these circumstances, a conditional discharge sums up the probation officer's assessment that there is no need for intervention and the case should be handled in the most lenient way possible. Second, the formulation may take a rather different form in that a conditional discharge is seen to be the most meaningful disposal for the offender. For example, a professional woman was charged with shop-lifting, the probation officer decided that she was not under personal or social stress at the time, and concluded that a conditional discharge would be a reminder of the jeopardy in which she had put herself and her job, commenting: 'I did not want her to be dealt with in a very punitive way and a conditional discharge would have a meaningful effect, especially for someone who is not used to going to court.' In this sense, a conditional discharge is seen, within the context of a person's needs, as a disposal which will remind an offender of the 'court's continuing presence'.

Fine

This disposal illustrates some of the ways in which a formulation either cancels out the relevance of identified needs, or relates a financial penalty specifically to a person's needs. For example, a youth was charged with a first offence of theft of lead and copper wire. He had had certain stresses in his early life such as going into care when his parents separated. However, the probation officer weighed up whether to recommend a fine or probation order and commented:

> When I started off doing the interviews for the report, things immediately started clicking when I found a disturbed background . . . Then I started asking different sorts of questions as I was investigating whether in fact there was any need for something like probation. After interviewing him and considering the situation, I felt it was not needed and recommended a a fine.

Such a formulation can only be reached once the relevant information has been acquired, studied and assessed.

In another case, a man was charged with theft, had a long criminal record, and the probation officer found it difficult to formulate an assessment. He was seriously considering a probation order but thought that would only, 'encourage a state of dependency in him because he likes to get others to assume responsibility for him'. The other factor that influenced the officer away from probation was that the offender had a link with his family and felt it preferable and appropriate to encourage a voluntary contact. It may seem strange to recommend a fine for someone in financial need! It is not so strange once the basis of the formulation has been identified. Accordingly, a fine may be recommended because either needs are minimal or they are already being met.

Probation

It is quite difficult to separate out those cases in which probation is recommended on the basis of need alone without any reference to a possible custodial sentence. However, though it is only a matter of degree, need often seems to be the overwhelming factor in the recommendations for probation. For example, a married man was charged with theft, resulting from an offence in which he had embezzled several hundred pounds from his laundry round. The probation officer came to a definite formulation that probation was indicated for the following reasons:

He had personal and social problems, wanted help and there-fore would respond to probation. He is a very isolated person and at this time was unemployed and seemed to be a bit workshy. He felt rejected by his family and was living in lodgings.

Sometimes the formulation may turn on probation as an anti-custody plea. For example, a young man was charged with criminal damage. He had previous criminal convictions and was on borstal licence. He had a very stressful history which included the tragic death of his girlfriend, a physical injury, a road accident and the death of his baby. The probation officer formulated his assessment as follows:

I did not want him to return to borstal. He was married, working and had a retrievable situation. His personality and attitudes were things we might discuss and affect through a probation order. I did not want to break up his marriage but to help them build up their relationship. His previous criminal record of violence also indicated that he obviously required help.

Needs are an important factor in the balance sheet whenever probation is recommended either as a straight supervision measure or a non-custodial alternative.

Custody

Sometimes, an offender's needs may be so overwhelming that either custody is seen to be inevitable—the end of the road—or an institutional measure is seen to hold some hope of helping a person with problems. For example, a young man was charged with six offences relating to damage and trespass, and had several previous convictions resulting in probation and borstal training. The probation officer concluded that custody was inevitable because,

his personality is so damaged that it cannot be easily or even completely repaired, and his offences were acting-out behaviour of what was going on in the home—partly a way to get back at his parents and life in general.

Quite apart from any risk to the community, a custodial sentence was seen to be necessary in order to protect the man from himself.

However, the formulation that an institution is necessary may be seen in a rather more positive light. For example, an adolescent boy with several previous convictions, already on probation, was charged with theft. His probation officer thought about persevering with probation but he had three overlapping orders in recent years. He summed up his formulation in the following way:

61

My reason for recommending a detention centre was that it was really a shot in the dark. By actually doing something and punishing him he would have to realise that something was happening to him and he might be put off. As he thinks he is bad, perhaps we can sort of purge it by making him pay for it. Therefore, taking his personality into account, I thought a detention centre would be a significant cause and effect thing for him. His record was also relevant because he was saying, 'I do not know why I do it, there I am and it happens and I do it'. Detention centre would help him think about it. Finally, the sentencing policy of the court came into it because I did not want them to go the whole hog and send him away to borstal or into care. I did not see the necessity for removing him because the basics were there in the family.

In some cases, the very 'stability' of an offender may be a positive indicator to the probation officer that an institutional measure might be appropriate. For example, a youth was jointly charged with theft as trespasser (involving several hundred pounds) and had one previous conviction. The probation officer thought that this was a serious and calculated offence, and, of even more importance, that he was a fairly stable young man who would not have been damaged by a detention centre experience; he might well benefit from it at that point. He needed a 'shock' because he had been able to go his own way for quite a while.

It seems from these examples, that probation officers sometimes see institutions as an 'end-of-the-road' resource, or, in a more positive light, as a place where an offender can get help.

Need does seem to be a factor in social inquiry assessments. Where need is minimal, conditional discharge may be indicated, where there are problems, probation may be suggested, whereas institutional measures may be necessary in cases of severe difficulty.

Resources

Probation officers also formulate their assessments within the context of available resources.

Conditional discharge

This may be a disposal that is reached not because there is no need or risk, but because the appropriate resources are not available. For example, a subnormal youth was charged with theft of lingerie. The probation officer considered probation, but concluded:

I was not sure whether we could usefully intervene or not. I tried to weigh up the use of probation in terms of limited resources; whether a probation officer's time could usefully be put to intervening in this case and I felt in the end that it probably would not help him make a great deal of progress. This was because of his low IQ and the things that go with that: lack of verbal ability and inability to examine and express his own feelings; inability to persist and concentrate indicated that behaviour therapy would not be appropriate.

Resources available elsewhere in the welfare system are also taken into account in the formulation of some assessments. For example, a woman was charged with assault following a domestic quarrel. The probation officer was considering a probation order but social services were already involved. She still wondered if the social work intervention was sufficient but concluded that:

the social worker's frequency and level of contact seemed to be sufficient and would not diminish in the future because there were good grounds for feeling anxiety about the well-being of the children.

Similar arguments are used in some cases of mentally disordered offenders. Once the probation officer is satisfied that there is sufficient support from the medical, social and psychiatric services, he might decide against probation and recommend a conditional discharge.

Fines

Resources are often relevant to fines because these disposals are sometimes chosen after a process of elimination. This happens in its simplest form when it is decided that a probation order should be kept in reserve for possible future occasions, and a fine is one way of achieving that. However the formulation is more complex in some cases. For example, an adolescent boy from a tinker family was jointly charged with theft. He was already on supervision and his probation officer wanted to continue with that. However, she found it difficult to come to a conclusion, saying,

I think that fines for juveniles are pretty pointless because the parents end up paying them and the kids get the brunt of it. It was a question of working out what was the least drastic thing that could happen to him. There was very little alternative because he had previously had a conditional discharge, two supervision orders and an attendance centre order the last time for a more serious offence when he might have gone to detention

63

centre. By a process of elimination, a fine seemed about the only thing because I wanted him to continue on supervision.

Often then, the formulation turns on a fine after alternative disposals have been eliminated.

Probation

Sometimes, the resources and preferences of a probation officer may lead to a formulation that probation is indicated even though the risk and need are not very serious. For example, a youth was charged with carrying an offensive weapon. The probation officer argued as follows:

> I obviously felt a probation order would help John at that particular time and he indicated he would like this. I was not going to press it because his needs were not terribly great and I wanted him to accept it so that we could have a good relationship rather than an authoritarian one. John related to me very positively whilst he was in prison. I was a nice mother image and he did have this need for an adult relationship. He had obvious practical difficulties including somewhere to live. The magistrates might not realise what I was getting at and think that probation was a little bit too severe for this offence. They like to find a positive way of dealing with the case, especially with the youngsters and they made a probation order. This is the kind of case which we take on in our office and my caseload was not too heavy at that time.

Therefore, probation may be a positive resource in a case which might otherwise be discharged. But when probation officers formulate their assessments in this way, they need to be aware of the issues of justice and due process involved.

Custody

Probation officers are often caught in a conflict, because in some cases they think an offender would benefit from some form of institutional treatment, but their professional experience of institutions leads them to doubt their efficacy. Sometimes, an institutional measure is positively recommended in the hope that a place will be available by the time of the court hearing. For example, a twenty-one-year-old man, already on probation, was charged with possessing an offensive weapon. Things had not been going well for him at home, he had been turned out by his family and was living in lodgings. The probation officer concluded that he still needed help with his alcoholism and personality problems, and was 'currently motivated towards making a better effort and expressed an interest in living in a hostel'. She thought that such a 'supportive and slightly structured environment might provide the means by which he could face up to his difficulties'. There was no bail hostel in the area so the offender was remanded in custody whilst a hostel place was found. Once this was done, probation was recommended with a clause that he should reside in a hostel for one year.

A variety of institutional measures is available for offenders, and knowledge of these and their availability will often influence the formulation the probation officer reaches.

Resources are an important feature of any formulation, in terms of either sentences available or possibilities for intervention and treatment. But resources are usually considered in terms of the risks and needs evident in a particular case.

Balancing risk, need and resources

In most of the cases described above, either risk, or need or resource was the outstanding factor underlying the assessment formulated. Some of the ways in which all three factors are systematically considered together as the probation officer formulates his assessment will now be illustrated.

Conditional discharge

A married woman was charged with theft of goods of small value from a store. The probation officer weighed up risk, need and resource in the following way:

I did not feel that Mrs Hope was showing signs of dishonesty, she would not really need a sanction, but some punishment because she would see her offence as wrong; the court appearance and conditional discharge is one way of acknowledging her conscience and that she had done something wrong. Also it means that there is no burden on her afterwards as long as she does not get into trouble again, which I think is extremely unlikely. [Risk]

There were several needs in this family which made me think about probation. There was a pattern of family disturbance and a chronic marital situation with some physical violence. Mrs Hope was also poorly; she had just had a hysterectomy and has had nervous trouble. Mr Hope had also had trouble with his nerves and feels depressed and insecure about his current unemployment. Even so, the Hope family is a closely-knit one where love, affection, problems and stresses are all shared.

Their adolescent daughter seems to have been affected by this and was acting out her problems at school. [Need]

There were several reasons why I recommended conditional discharge rather than probation. Originally both Mrs Hope and her daughter were going to be jointly charged; I wrote the two reports, and recommended supervision for Mary thinking that this would provide an avenue for working with the whole family; in the event, the charges against the girl were dropped. In this sense my plan back-fired, though I have seen Mrs Hope and Mary on a voluntary basis since the court appearance. Also, social services had agreed to offer help anyway, so they were going to be covered. I recommended a conditional discharge because a fine would have been a tremendous burden to Mrs Hope. For some people in this sort of situation it helps them to be able to pay a fine because they feel better paying something for what they have done. But I ruled this out. [Resources]

The risk was low, needs were evident, but resources were available from social services in this complex conditional discharge case, which seemed to be a probation-inevitable one on the surface.

Fine

A man was charged with criminal damage and had about thirty previous convictions, several custodial sentences and was currently on probation. The probation officer's overwhelming aim in recommending a fine was to keep the man out of prison. His formulation was as follows:

I have had such a long involvement with Jim. He is still a very great risk but I have been relatively successful with him. He has not actually been to prison for three years now which is marvellous compared with his previous record. I think he is a diminishing risk, but there is still that element there. [Risk]

I think Jim is a psychopathological character. He has a disturbed childhood, is divorced, has an erratic work record and needs help with his personal and social problems, he is currently working and living in a stable cohabitation. [Need]

I did not worry too much what happened as long as he did not go to prison. I did not spell out a fine because I wanted to give the court their own range of sentence. I indicated that Jim would be well able to pay a fine. I was very conscious that I had to fight the likely sentencing policy of the court which meant that he had every chance of going to prison. [Resources]

Therefore, the formulation here was that Jim was at risk but things were getting better, his needs were diminishing, the likelihood of a custodial sentence had to be argued against, but resources were available through an existing probation order.

Probation

A man was charged with several offences of incest. This offence is usually considered very seriously in courts and results in a custodial sentence. In this case, however, the probation officer argued for probation, after taking into account risk, need and resources. Such offences rarely come to public notice, but in this case, the twelve-year-old daughter involved had been behaving rather difficultly at school and stealing. The teacher reported her to the police, when she mentioned the offences. The assessment was formulated in the following way:

> The public's reaction to this kind of offence is one of horror and disgust; I do not have such a moralistic view, especially since I have had contact with several people who have been in-volved in such offences. My main concern was what it had done to the girl in terms of her age and emotionally. There will be no possibility that the offences will be repeated because no contact will be permitted between Mr Brown and his daughter. [Risk]
>
> I felt Mr Brown needed help. He is a naïve and gullible person with a low IQ. He has been deprived of a secure family life coupled with unsettled institutional care. (If he had been in one foster home all his life that would have ruled out the negative effect.) He considers that he has a high sex drive and lacks internal self controls. There were problems in the family, be-cause of his wife's infidelity and the collusion that went on. [Need]
>
> From a social work point of view, I knew he needed help and I knew we could offer him that sort of help whether or not it would be effective. I knew a probation order was possible because in my previous experience the court had made one in an incest case. This led me to believe it was worth sticking my neck out but I knew I was sticking it out a long way. I thought I was justified even at the risk of losing some credibility. I think the court on the whole does take a fairly moralistic and fairly unrealistic line. It takes the view that this sort of thing needs to be deterred and a hefty prison sentence will deter it, which I think is rubbish. I made sure that there was someone in the treatment team who was willing to take this case on, and there was. [Resources]

The formulation stage here was a very complex process of weighing up the low risk of reoffending, the man's evident needs, and the resources available through a probation order.

Custody

Sometimes, probation officers make positive recommendations for custody. For example, a young man was charged with burglary, had numerous previous convictions and had been on probation several times. He was recommended for borstal training and the probation officer formulated his assessment in this way:

> Alf was charged with burglary, but he had actually committed several offences round about the same time. He was at risk anyway because he was very unsettled, homeless and he had stolen to get food, I thought he was at risk of committing further offences if he stayed in the community, was not living at home and going round with people who get into trouble and a point had been reached when society needed some protection. [Risk]
>
> His needs were overwhelming. He has been a problem since he was four and there may be some congenital abnormality there. He looks strange, has thick glasses and his eyes discharge. He is not very bright and started stealing within the home at an early age; his mother became very, very protective towards him and was standing between him and father who was a very strict disciplinarian. He has a haphazard work record too. His father eventually threw him out and he moved around from place to place. He was also clinically depressed, had attempted suicide and was receiving psychiatric treatment. Altogether, he had so many needs which were crying out for help. [Need]
>
> I could have continued with probation but he had had three tries and I did not feel that I had anything positive to tell the court. There seemed to be no chance that he could return home. Therefore, several things made me think that borstal could be a positive thing for him. I thought I could work with the family whilst he was in borstal, so that if they were reasonably positive about it when he came out, they would accept him back; it would be a very positive thing for him to be back with his family because he desperately needed his mother in particular and felt rejection from father. He had actually been asking to go to borstal too, especially during his depressive phases because his very close friend had gone to borstal; but he also felt he needed to be punished and purged for his sins. I did worry about how he would get on in borstal because of his strange looks. He could have been rejected and suffered quite a

lot there. In the end, I concluded that this was a situation he faced every day anyway and at least he might be helped to deal with these problems in borstal. I felt that detention centre would be absolutely impossible and would not touch him at all, as he did not need a punitive approach. In the end, therefore, I thought that borstal was a positive step, which would help him with his problems and that he would benefit from this.
[Resources]

Borstal was thus seen as a positive resource for Alf who was at risk, and had many problems, some of which could be dealt with either directly or indirectly in that environment.

As probation officers formulate their assessments in social inquiries, they usually weigh up risk, need and resource; sometimes one cancels out the other, whereas in other cases, the equation indicates that intervention seems to be appropriate. Whatever equations probation officers reach, they should share them with the offenders concerned, so that the conclusion to the report comes as no surprise to them.

A tariff in reverse

There is some evidence (Hardiker 1977b, 1978) that there may be some underlying principles behind the assessments which probation officers formulate. It is important to explore these principles in relation to practice theory, because the case illustrations presented above may give an impression that the equations made were relatively *ad hoc* or idiosyncratic. Systematic evidence from a large sample of cases (*ibid.*) suggests that this is not the case.

Martin Davies (1971, 18) originally hypothesised that social inquiry reports indicated:

> where on the continuum of social need the offender stands. If the need is minimal, a fine or conditional discharge will be recommended. If problems exist, then a probation order is made. If problems are severe, or previous probation has failed, custodial measures are considered.

Davies called this a 'tariff system in reverse'. Whilst the hypothesis is very important, because (as we have seen) 'need' is a significant factor in the formulation of any assessment it seems to oversimplify the situation. For example, a conditional discharge or fine may be recommended in some high need cases, because either the risk is low or the offender is already getting help from other resources; sometimes, probation is still recommended in cases where there are severe problems or previous probation has failed. Davies's hypothesis therefore needs to be revised.

The evidence (Hardiker, 1977b) suggests that other factors in addition to need form an essential part of any social inquiry assessment. These may be described as either 'tariff' or 'risk', and indicate that the relative seriousness of the offender's current offence(s) and previous criminal history is given some consideration at the formulation stage. The revised reverse tariff hypothesis therefore, reads:

> The sentencer through the medium of the social inquiry report determines *where on the continuum of tariff and social need the offender stands*. If the tariff and need are minimal, a conditional discharge will be recommended; if the tariff is moderate and needs are minimal, a fine will be indicated; if the tariff is moderate and needs are evident, probation will be suggested; a maximum tariff and serious personal and social problems will be a pointer to custodial measures (Hardiker, 1977b, p. 22).

As we have seen, risk and need are often considered together in social inquiries, and need on its own may not be the only factor which is given priority in an assessment. For example, the fact that Alf was thought to be at risk and that society needed some protection from him was a very significant factor in the probation officer's recommendation for borstal training.

The formulation may also hinge on the availability of appropriate resources, Jim's probation officer was well aware that risk and need were still relatively serious, but his recommendation for a fine as a non-custodial alternative was made in the knowledge that sufficient resources would continue to be available through the existing probation order. Even though Mr Brown, who was charged with incest, was in very great need, it was thought that the probation service could provide adequate resources to meet those needs.

There is statistical evidence available elsewhere (Hardiker, 1977b) to provide substance to these generalisations, because it is never sufficient to rest an argument on isolated case illustrations. The idea of the 'reverse tariff' plus some consideration of the resource factor appears to be a relatively precise way of describing the formulation stage in any social inquiry and can be illustrated in a table.

Conditional discharge will tend to be recommended in cases where the offence is relatively trivial (low tariff) and there is no evidence of need (low need). If the offence is rather more serious (medium tariff) and there are few needs, a fine will probably be recommended, whereas probation will be suggested in similar cases if there are evidence needs (medium tariff/high need). Custody is more likely if the offences are serious (high tariff) and needs seem to be very evident. This simple formula does not exhaust the parameters of

A Reverse Tariff

Need	Tariff		
	Low	*Medium*	*High*
Low	*Conditional discharge*	*Fine*	
High	(Conditional discharge)	*Probation* (Fine)	*Custody* (Probation)

recommendations. As can be seen from the diagram, conditional discharge and fine may sometimes be suggested in high need cases, and probation might be tried again even in serious high tariff/high need situations.

The case of Mr Smith (Chapter one) may be considered in terms of the 'tariff in reverse'. This was assessed as a *high need* case, in view of Mr Smith's family and financial problems, his 'inadequately developed personality', and his difficulty in sustaining regular employment. His offences were also relatively serious (thefts valued at several hundred pounds). Because of these and his previous conviction, it was felt that Mr Smith was a *medium/high risk* as he tended to solve his financial problems by criminal means. The resources of the probation service through a probation order were available and seemed to be appropriate given risks and needs in this case. If Mr Smith had not had so many problems, a fine might have been considered, or if he had problems but resources had not been available, some form of custodial sentence might have been recommended. But, risk, need and resource considered together, led to the formulation that probation seemed appropriate.

We would like to suggest that the 'reverse tariff' is an important element in implicit practice theories rather than explicit theories of practice in social inquiry assessments. Probation officers internalise various feelings and ideas about 'tariff' and 'need' and rank these fairly implicitly as they formulate their assessments in each case. For example, the respective probation officers thought that Mrs Hope was 'unlikely to get into trouble again', 'Jim was a psychopathological character', 'Mr Brown was naïve and gullible', 'Alf felt he needed to be punished and purged for his sins by going to borstal'. These measures of risk, need and resource are not codified anywhere as explicit theories of probation practice. They are sets of ideas which probation officers have worked out for themselves in relation to the offenders with whom they deal. They partly rest on social science ideas (for example, psychopathology), and social work methods (for example, need for help) but they also reflect certain value premises and 'common-sense' observations about such things as the likelihood that a woman will not re-offend or what the magistrates will tolerate.

The evidence on the 'reverse tariff' basis of social inquiry assessments has been gathered as part of an independent sociological investigation of probation officers' ideologies (*ibid*.). As Evans (1976) remarks, 'if we regard practice theory as valid knowledge, then our task is to help social workers conceptualise and codify what they do in practice and to incorporate this into our theory' (p. 195). In this chapter, we have attempted to codify some of the ways in which probation officers formulate their assessments and to conceptualise this in terms of a 'reverse tariff' hypothesis. If this is valid knowledge, then implicit practice theories could become part of explicit theories of practice in social inquiry reports. This would mean that probation officers would actively and explicitly formulate their assessments in terms of the reverse tariff equation, and be aware of the principles at stake if they opt for probation in high risk cases or suggest supervision when the tariff hardly justifies it. For example, if Mr Smith's probation officer was clear about the assessment he had formulated, and the principles underlying it, he perhaps should have spelled out to the court more precisely the reason why he felt risk and need were high, but containable within a probation order. There is no reason why sentencers should always agree with probation officers' recommendations but there are good reasons for suggesting that social inquiry reports should spell out the principles underlying the assessment of risk, need and resource in a relatively explicit way—that is, if we regard practice theory as valid knowledge.

Chapter five

Skills and methods in setting goals

In previous chapters we have discussed the process of acquiring and studying information and producing a balance sheet at the formulation stage. We have indicated the limitations, boundaries and focus of the worker's activity at each of these stages, whilst acknowledging that the phases of the assessment process overlap and impinge on each other and are not discrete sequences. We come now to the goal-setting phase as the final stage of the assessment model under consideration.

Social work is a shared, planned and purposeful activity in relation to the definition of a problem and some means of achieving objectives in relation to it. Sometimes there will be full agreement between the worker and the client about the identified problem and the ways in which it can be alleviated. In other instances the worker and client may agree to differ in their interpretation of the situation and about how, or whether, it should be changed.

Goal-setting

Three crucial points should be borne in mind at the goal-setting stage. First, the recommendation that is made in the report is not the goal of the assessment, but it is the means by which the goal is specified for the court hearing through the report that is presented. Second, we have indicated in previous chapters how important the sharing of information and opinion between worker and client is at all stages; it is particularly important at the goal-setting stage for the sharing to be confined to the assessment conclusion rather than to the intervention plans. This means that the goal will be to decide whether or not the need for a particular kind of intervention has been agreed upon and to ask for this in court.

This leads us to the third point, that the goal as set out in the report can be legitimated only by the court and not by the other people involved in the assessment. The worker, in considering what the goal should be, is not working as a free and independent agent but has to work within the context and limitations of his role in relation to the court and the sentencers. Accordingly, his work must be directed towards making clear to the court the relevant evidence for his recommendation for the particular method of intervention or non-intervention.

The focus of the activity during assessment is on the client in his particular situation, and the worker attempts to express his professional view and understanding of this combination of factors. He considers the extent to which the problems reside within the client or whether they originate elsewhere yet affect the client's behaviour and responses. The conclusions he reaches contribute to the balance sheet which must then be considered in relation to the court's expectations and demands, given the set of circumstances with which it is presented. The goal that is recommended must be seen as appropriate and relevant to the court; even if it is not agreed by the offender, the reasoning which informed the conclusion, must be understood by him. It is evidence of poor practice by the worker if he has indicated to a client that he intends to recommend one sentence to the court but ends up suggesting a different disposal in his report, without explaining and sharing with the offender the reasons for the change of plan.

This problem often arises in cases where the offence and previous criminal record are so serious that the court is likely to give a custodial sentence. In these 'custody-inevitable' cases, the worker has a responsibility to make clear to the offender that the seriousness of the situation and the likely outcome will be acknowledged in the social inquiry report. This works the other way round too. If a custodial sentence seems inevitable, but the probation officer has set some goals with the client which imply a non-custodial intervention, he must share with the offender that he will write a 'strategic' anti-custody report to the court. As we have seen, probation officers may accept, argue against or work with the sentencing policy of the court. Whatever direction their work takes, they should share and set their goals with their clients.

Goal-setting is concerned with the decision as to whether a particular kind of social work help is needed. The need for intervention can be met through a variety of sentences besides probation, as when a fine is recommended as a means of enabling an offender to continue under supervision. This is one reason why the recommendation cannot be equated with the goal; a variety of sentences can be recommended as a means of indicating the need for intervention, and the same apparent recommendation can be made to support many different goals. This is perfectly appropriate activity for the probation officer, provided that the specific and bounded nature of the goals set at the assessment stage is recognised.

Recommendations in social inquiry reports are a controversial issue in the literature (Ford, 1972; Hardiker, 1975; The Morison Report, 1962; Perry, 1974; The Streatfeild Report, 1961). The debate cannot be analysed here, but the evidence indicates that probation officers in fact make recommendations in about eighty per cent of their social inquiry reports. This must have implications for social work processes in such assessments generally and goal-setting specifically.

Intake systems may be one way in which probation officers are helped through organisational measures to think more clearly about these issues (Hardiker, 1977b). First, the workers must distinguish between the assessment and intervention stages of the social work process, and this may help them to make more objective assessments. Second, they may feel it necessary to keep their credibility with their colleagues in the long-term teams, and this forces them to think more diagnostically about the need for probation supervision. Third, they must negotiate resources and facilities with the long-term teams, who may not have the capacity to supervise another offender. These may be some of the reasons why recommendations for probation decreased in one agency which started an intake system (*ibid.*). They show up again the importance of organisational contexts in social work assessments.

Assessment and intervention compared

The various stages of the assessment process—acquisition, study, formulation and goal-setting—are not neat, orderly sequences which follow on from each other. They are complex stages which overlap. Similarly, the assessment and intervention stages in social work may not be the neat and orderly sequences we have outlined. But it is essential for social workers to understand the differences between these stages of their work and to maintain an analytical distinction between them in their practice because assessment and intervention often merge both empirically and temporally. First, relationships and interaction between the worker and client begin at the start of most assessments, but this can only be described as intervention in a very loose and broad sense. (We are not concerned in this book to debate the arguments based on psycho-dynamic theories and assumptions about the special and therapeutic nature of the 'social work relationship'; see Sainsbury, 1970 and Yelloly, 1972, for a fuller discussion of these issues). Second, sometimes workers have to intervene in order to assess, and sometimes their very assessments may bring about some change. Third, assessments will be revised throughout any intervention. Fourth, sometimes immediate needs may be met at the assessment stage, especially when practical help is required. Fifth, crisis intervention may be achieved during a social inquiry, and in these circumstances the stages we have specified will be telescoped. Nevertheless, the special nature of goal-setting in social inquiries needs to be conceptualised, analysed and understood and this can be done by confining this stage of work to the assessment for the court (or case conference). Most contracts and goals in relation to the intervention phase of work should be delayed until either the sentence has been passed or the assessment has been ratified by relevant people in the case.

We are aware of particular situations in inquiries in which probation officers would argue that the model presented in regard to the goal-setting stage is neither appropriate nor accurate. One such situation is when the inquiry relates to a juvenile client. Monger argues that, whereas with adults the probation officer's role is to assist the court in reaching a decision (Monger, 1972), with juveniles it is inappropriate to expect to create an atmosphere where help is acceptable and then to withdraw it until after the court hearing (Monger, 1974). Two points seem to be worth comment here. First, juveniles are more dependent than adults on the significant people in their environment, and the help that can be offered to them can only be effective if it is also acceptable to those people. The young person also is less able to understand help that comes and goes and could well find it difficult to respond if the continuity with the worker offering help is broken. Second, the court's welfare sanction is more predominant in the case of children and young people than it is with adults.

The second situation where probation officers may feel that the goal-setting stage more nearly merges into intervention is where a remand or pre-trial period is protracted because the offender is awaiting an appearance in the crown court. There may be differing views as to how this should be faced by the worker. One may be to compare it with the longer assessment period of the custody inquiry and to use it primarily for working out with all concerned what the goal should be. Another view would be that it is a period that can be used to test out the validity and feasibility of what has been seen as the goal, so that the recommendation can then be made with greater certainty. This may be particularly pertinent where social work intervention is the goal. Therefore, probation officers will usually want to do some work with an offender during a protracted remand period, and this will be perfectly appropriate, provided the specific and bounded nature of his task and purpose is clear to the parties involved.

Even allowing for the special situations described above, probation officers do not necessarily adhere to the requirements of the assessment/intervention model which has been outlined. First, they sometimes either confuse or telescope the assessment, intervention and evaluation stages of their work. Second, they may not always share their assessments with offenders. Third, the goals they set are not always specifiable and attainable. Fourth, a social work process model may not be applicable to every social inquiry situation. However, good social inquiry practice should be facilitated if social workers are clear about the special nature of goal-setting, the boundaries of social inquiry recommendations and the analytical distinctions between assessment, intervention and evaluation.

Analysis of goal-setting

Work at the goal-setting stage proceeds on the basis of the analysis made earlier, as information has been acquired and studied and a balance sheet drawn up at the formulation stage. Goal-setting relates particularly to the balance of risk, need and resource which has been formulated.

Many factors have to be taken into account if the need for social work intervention is the agreed-upon goal. The offender's personal and social needs are examined in relation to how they may be met by social work help. The person's strengths are considered, especially in relation to whether he knows how to use resources and requires assistance to do so, or whether his ability to meet different demands is such that he can respond appropriately or has to learn other ways of becoming more acceptable in his closer or wider environment. There has also to be an assessment of the person's motivation to accept help. The worker looks for evidence or otherwise that the client has been able previously to use help, or has never been given the opportunity of help, or that the help offered previously has not been either appropriate or sufficient. The worker examines what help is currently accessible to the client and, if other services of either a social, medical, preventive or promotional nature are on hand, considers whether help through a probation or supervision order can materially add anything for the client. The officer assesses whether the personality of the offender is either too damaged or too complex to respond to the help that he or his service can offer. This factor is also linked with the officer's view of how far his agency, because of the limitations of its function or its resources can offer help to the person in his particular personal and social situation. The worker also considers whether or not he, or one of his colleagues, and the offender can work together to achieve change. Finally, the worker must bear in mind as the background to all the above considerations what the risk would be of offering social work help because of either the previous criminal history, the seriousness of the current offence or the likelihood of continuing offending behaviour.

We shall now examine, with the use of some case illustrations, some of the varied goals which probation officers set in their social inquiry work.

1 Intervention not indicated—straightforward

Social inquiry reports are frequently prepared on offenders who are not in a situation of personal and social need and for whom social work intervention is not indicated. In such cases, a recommendation for either a conditional discharge or a fine—depending on the relative triviality of the offence and previous record—will be a means of giving an expression to this goal. For example, a young boy with his friend stole some oranges from outside a shop. This was the boy's first offence, and neither the officer nor the court viewed it as serious. The boy came from a stable home where the parents showed concern for their children. They had already indicated their displeasure to the boy at acting foolishly. The home was not in a high risk area in terms of delinquent peer group pressures, and the boy received an adequate report from school. The boy showed regret at the bother his offence had caused and displayed normal concern about his court appearance but was not overwhelmed by it once he knew the possible outcome. Given these circumstances, a recommendation for conditional discharge seemed appropriate, since further intervention was not indicated.

2 Probation intervention not indicated—social services involved.*

Social inquiry reports are sometimes prepared on offenders who are already under the supervision of either the probation or social services department. Usually, the goal in these circumstances is to ensure that the court gives a sentence which will enable supervision to continue, because an additional supervision order is deemed unnecessary. A recommendation for either a conditional discharge or fine—depending on the tariff—will be a means of giving expression to this goal.

For example, a twenty-two-year-old married woman, the mother of two children, was charged with assault occasioning actual bodily harm, an offence which had arisen during a domestic dispute. The probation officer concluded that though this was a high need case, intervention through a probation order was not required because of

*The social inquiry report presented in this case is outlined in Appendix II/A.

the level of contact which the family had with the social services department. Her recommendation for a conditional discharge was a means of giving expression to this goal.

Acquisition of information

The probation officer used the client as the main source of information, and saw her with her children and the husband. There were no records to obtain confirmation of the client's account of her difficult and disrupted childhood. Clarification of the current family difficulties was sought, with the client's knowledge, from the worker in the social services department. The probation officer was careful to show her understanding about how the woman might feel about accepting help, because of her previous contact with social work agencies. The woman's personal, social and cultural norms were also considered because they affected the way the worker and client communicated. The worker also had to keep the focus of her inquiry on the offence, even though she identified many signs of stress in the woman's life. These circumstances had to be explored because they gave meaning to the offence behaviour, but the probation officer made sure that she did not lose the focus of her work or overstep the boundary of her assessment work.

Study

The frameworks which the probation officer used to make sense of this case were based within a 'treatment' context. The offence was considered in an individualised way rather than on the tariff. The assault had arisen from a domestic dispute between the offender and her sister-in-law, following suspicions that the latter had made allegations against the defendant's care of her children. The probation officer contextualised the offence within the family's norms of appropriate behaviour and accepted the defendant's interpretation of it. There were many factors in the offender's life which had to be studied. The family situation indicated some stresses; the welfare and health of the children was a matter of concern because an older child had died the previous year, and a social worker was currently working with the children and their mother. The marriage seemed stable, but there were financial pressures, especially because the husband was currently unemployed. The family's current lack of resources, the poor material conditions in the home and rent arrears seemed to be tied up with the husband's irregular employment arising from his trade rather than from the couple's personal inadequacies. Generally, stresses outweighed strengths in this family. The court was likely to see the case in a similar way.

Formulation

The balance sheet was quite complex in this case. The risk in relation to the offence seemed low, once it was seen in the context of the offender's family as a fierce quarrel. However, risk in relation to the children's welfare had to be considered, because the standard of child care was low. There were also risks, given the family's poor financial circumstances. This was a high need case, because of the welfare of the children, the financial situation, the housing position, the employment problems and economic circumstances, the offender's personal needs and family relationships. But these risks and needs had to be weighed up in relation to resources. The risk to the children and their needs within their family were being adequately dealt with by the local authority social worker. However, the officer thought that the other needs in the situation could not be met through a probation order. The family was already receiving the benefits due to them so a probation order could neither alleviate their financial problems nor their housing situation. The offender seemed to be coping with the demands and pressures on her and she appeared to be responding to the help she was getting from the social worker.

Goal-setting

The goal was in terms of non-intervention for the probation service. The social inquiry report presented an assessment which supported that conclusion and the recommendation for a conditional discharge. The court was informed of the balance of risk and need and the resources already available to the family. A conditional discharge gave expression to these goals, as it could be seen as conveying to the client the confidence that the court and the officer had in her ability to cope with difficulties and to use what help was available from the local authority. It would also remind her that, though her offence behaviour might seem justified to her, it was against the law. A conditional discharge would be a more positive way of dealing with this offender than a fine because it conveyed a confidence the court and probation officer had that she was unlikely to get into trouble with the law again and put the onus on the defendant to behave within the law for a specified period. Put in these terms, the defendant should see a conditional discharge as helpful rather than punitive.

Assessment/intervention

The probation officer was clear about her assessment role during this inquiry. Even though the offence was to some extent concerned with family circumstances, the officer was careful not to become involved in these beyond the focus of the inquiry related to the offence. The worker specified needs in fairly precise terms, but assessed that, whilst some problems were being handled by another agency, the probation service could not help with the wider stresses in this family, and she was careful not to start on any loose and general long-term intervention plan.

3 Intervention not indicated—high need but unsuitable for probation.

Probation officers may identify needs at the social inquiry stage, but decide that probation is inappropriate because of the 'mental' condition of the offender, lack of motivation for help, beyond help because of either a damaged personality or the seriousness of the situation. For example, a middle-aged woman was charged with assault occasioning actual bodily harm. She had no previous convictions and was said to be suffering from schizophrenia. The probation officer thought that the woman would not be able to respond to the techniques of probation supervision; as she was already receiving psychiatric help, further· action of a punitive nature was inappropriate; therefore, a conditional discharge was recommended. When the situation is more serious because of either the offender's damaged personality or the seriousness of the offence, the inevitability of a custodial sentence is usually acknowledged in the social inquiry report because probation seems inappropriate.

4 Social work intervention indicated—high need

The most straightforward cases are those in which social work intervention through a probation order is indicated, given a balance sheet in which need is high, risks are moderate (or low) and resources are available. One such case concerned a young married couple who were jointly charged with stealing food to the value of under two pounds. At the time of the offence, they were in a desperate personal, financial and social situation.*

Acquisition

The first sources of information for the probation officer were the couple themselves as they appeared in court and a letter which the wife handed to the magistrates. The officer observed their demeanour

---

*The social inquiry report which was presented in this case is outlined in Appendix II/B.

and behaviour in court which indicated the anxiety and stress they were feeling. The letter indicated that the wife had previously attempted suicide and was in contact with a psychiatrist, and that there were signs of stress in the marital relationship. The officer continued to use the husband and wife as the main source of information, but he also acquired data from records relating to the wife's earlier probation order, the defending solicitor, and other statutory departments which were contacted, such as the psychiatrist who indicated that the wife suffered from depression. There were few barriers to communication because the couple were intelligent, articulate, motivated to seek help and anxious to discuss their problems. The wife had had earlier positive experiences of social work help; the husband had had no previous experience of courts or probation officers but responded to the obvious wish to alleviate their problems that the officer demonstrated. The couple were, therefore, willing to give information as requested about themselves and their circumstances, and sought relief of their personal and marital problems. The problems of communication at this stage arose from the paralysing stresses the couple were under, and the officer responded to their immediate needs whilst keeping his activities focused on the inquiry.

Study

The offence was seen as a trivial infringement of the law, but the way that it was committed (within view of other people) seemed to be a 'cry for help', and the probation officer studied it in an individualised way rather than on the tariff. Stresses seemed to outweigh strengths in the couple's situation; the wife was in poor physical and mental health, but the husband seemed healthy; the wife also seemed to have a basic need for support and dependence on others, but the husband was a more independent character who was able in normal circumstances to respond to his wife's needs. However, with the particular stresses of current low income, debts, his wife's illness, and his doubts about his ability to retain her affection, in addition to the anxiety about the offence and court appearance, he was less sure of his capacity to cope with the demands of marriage and adulthood. The couple were experiencing some difficulties within their marriage. Given these circumstances, the probation officer could be confident that the court would agree that the resources of probation should be mobilised for this couple.

Formulation

The balance sheet was fairly straightforward. The risk was low, because the offence was quite trivial and seemed to stem from the couple's current circumstances; if those circumstances improved, the likelihood of further offences was small. The probation officer realised that the risk was low because the court normally dealt with these cases by a fine. This was clearly a high need case, given the couple's personal difficulties, marital problems, poor health of the wife, and their poor financial resources. Resources had already been harnessed at the inquiry stage in order to meet the couple's immediate needs. Help was mobilised from the medical, psychiatric and voluntary services, payment of tax rebate was expedited, and arrangements were made with the electricity board about an outstanding bill. The couple still had many problems which needed further attention and could properly be relieved through the medium of a probation order, for which resources were available.

Goal-setting

The goal was fairly easily distinguishable because of the balance of risk, need and resource. There was little likelihood of the court seeing punishment as the outcome, and the need for social work intervention was so apparent. The goal was to communicate to the court that the couple needed help and that this was available in the probation service. The targets for help were clearly evident and could be specified to the court: marital problems, psychiatric difficulties, material and employment stress. The probation officer was also able to indicate to the court that the couple had already accepted and responded well to the help offered, so that they would be likely to respond to further social work intervention. Even though the offence was trivial, probation seemed appropriate because a conditional discharge would have indicated an authority-based control without offering them positive assistance through continuity of social work contact; a fine would have been an inappropriate punishment and would have added to their financial stress. The probation officer knew that the court would see the appropriateness of probation in this case.

Assessment/Intervention

It might be asked whether the officer was justified in giving so much social work help before the court had given him the authority to do so, but his justification lay in three areas. First, a crisis situation was recognised by the court when the wife's letter was read; they immediately wanted to involve the officer with that, and in so doing indicated an expectation of action to be taken during the assessment. Second, there were so many problems immediately apparent; though some of these were being dealt with by other agencies, there were other problems for which the couple were in need of urgent help and for which no other agency was involved. Third, the assessment process would have been seriously impeded or inaccurate if the immediate, short-term intervention had not taken place. The couple were so immobilised by their problems that until some relief was offered to them, their true capacity to use help and their motivation to change could not be assessed.

5 Intervention through institutional provision indicated

Sometimes, probation officers make positive recommendations for an institutional sentence because they have formulated that the offender needs either treatment or containment in a custodial setting. These settings may range from the relative openness of a probation hostel to the more closed setting of a prison, or a variety of detention centre and borstal provisions. A variety of goals may be set in these circumstances: deterrence of further criminal behaviour (Davies, 1973); the provision of a warm, enabling parental figure, given a youth's stage of development (Davies and Sinclair, 1971); the need for a 'short, sharp, shock' for a stable youth whose criminality has not been curbed by previous sentences (Box and Forde, 1971); training for a youth at a peak in his delinquent career; 'time-out' for an offender whose life is in shreds and who has been rejected by his family. Very often in these circumstances, the risk factor is important because of either the seriousness of the offences or the persistent criminality of the offender. But when positive recommendations are made for institutional measure, these are not simply an acknowledgment that 'custody is inevitable', but an attempt to set more specific goals for the offender. Risk and need are usually high in these circumstances, but it is felt that institutional resources can be used for rehabilitation purposes.

For example, a youth aged seventeen was charged with two offences of stealing cash; they were part of a series of many thefts from business premises, which the youth had committed individually and jointly with others over several months. The total value of goods and cash was about three thousand pounds. Within a few weeks of the current offence, the youth had been twice before the court, when first a probation order and then an attendance centre order were made. The goal-setting was very complex in this case.*

---

*The social inquiry report which was presented in this case is outlined in Appendix II/C.

Acquisition

The probation officer already had some information on the youth who was currently under his supervision. But it was necessary to collect information about the current offences and circumstances, and the probation officer used the youth himself as his main source of data. The youth's attitudes to the previous and current offences had to be explored, in order to identify their significance to him and whether they reflected changed circumstances. The officer also needed to find out from the police more about the scale and nature of the offences and to explore more fully the youth's family and social circumstances. There were likely to be barriers to communication because of the expectations that the youth would have about how the officer would view the much more serious nature of the offences. There were also cultural barriers to communication, because 'anti-social' behaviour was common on the estate where the youth lived, and authority-figures were viewed with suspicion. The probation officer realised that the youth might have found himself in a tight corner between peer-group pressures and family expectations, but it was necessary to individualise his situation. Some of these barriers were overcome during the inquiry, because the officer was able to communicate to the youth that he realised that the current charges were much more serious than the level of criminality he had assumed at the beginning of the probation order. The officer was also aware that the roles that he and the youth had assumed within the probation order had to change for the purpose of the current inquiry.

Study

The frameworks that were used to study this case were no different from those in a new inquiry. The focus had to be on the offences, the offender given his social circumstances, and the sentencing policy of the court. Though the offences were serious, the probation officer individualised them in relation to the youth's circumstances and saw them as an initial drift into crime out of an aimless and deteriorated work situation, which continued because his activities became so profitable. The offence made sense in terms of personal, family and social situation, even though their seriousness had to be acknowledged. There were both strengths and stresses in the offender's life. He lived with his younger brother and his paternal grandmother in a comfortable home where there were limited financial resources. He had been in this home since early childhood following his mother's desertion through a psychiatric breakdown, when his father was a serviceman abroad. He knew the facts of his home life from an early age, and was given, and accepted, good parental care by both grand-parents. The father remarried and retained contact with his sons. The grandfather died when the youth was fifteen. The probation officer studied the youth's disrupted early life but decided that it had not apparently adversely affected the boy. The youth was of average ability, had achieved well at school and had left early with a view to assuming some financial responsibility in the home following his grandfather's death. The youth worked first as an apprentice, then left this job because the money was insufficient, and then took three jobs in quick succession. He had been unemployed for three months prior to the inquiry, because his firm did not keep his job for him after he had been ill, following a football accident, and he had been unable to obtain other work. The probation officer weighed the strengths and stresses in this situation and thought that, despite unusual background circumstances, the youth was a balanced young man who had no more personal problems than those of normal adolescents. The death of his grandfather seemed to have had some bearing on the youth's drift into crime, because he had previously been a law-abiding person in a 'delinquent' area. His drift into crime was also associated with his unemployment, but he had used his intelligence to carry out serious offences over a period of time in a deliberate and calculated way. There were stresses in his situation and the youth's very strengths were aiding his criminal career. The court would view the case very seriously. The probation officer also had to acknowledge that the youth's co-operation during the supervision order must have been superficial, given the scale of his concurrent criminal activities which were later revealed. The re-sources of probation did not seem to have had any influence on the youth's motivation to change. Therefore, the serious offences were seen as calculated risks, given the offender's circumstances, and the probation officer decided that probation was inappropriate at that stage.

Formulation

The balance sheet hinged heavily on risks in this case. The offences were serious and calculated; the youth lived in a 'delinquent' neighbourhood and was unemployed; he was unlikely to obtain employment at the time of the inquiry, and it was in seeking employment (or pretending to do so) that he had gained access to business premises. The risk of re-offending was very high, especially as the youth lacked the strength of a firm, male, parental figure in his home. There were needs in this youth's situation too. The most striking need seemed to be for guidance and encouragement from a strong, male adult whom he could respect. He also needed training and preparation for employment, so that he could settle down and make his contribution to the home which was and would continue to be, an important anchor and support to him. The youth also needed help to resist the peer-group pressures where he lived, so that he could make more independent choices about his criminal and other activities. Given this scale of risk and need, the probation officer had to decide whether resources should be based in an institution or in the community. If community resources were to be made available, something more was needed than the probation and attendance centre orders because these seemed to have made little impact on the youth. It was unlikely that the court would agree to a new probation order, because they had a responsibility to prevent other offences as well as to punish the youth for his persistent criminal behaviour. A probation order with a condition of residence in a hostel might have been appropriate, but such resources were limited and the risk was probably too high. The youth needed training and guidance and the opportunity to get into regular work habits. Borstal resources would be available but their effectiveness as a training opportunity and preparation for work was more suspect. The youth could go to a neighbourhood borstal where his links with home would be maintained. He would also meet there people from his neighbourhood, so his ability to deal with pressure from them would be tested out under surveillance. A further advantage of borstal would be that he would get through-care and after-care contact with the probation service. However, borstal seemed inappropriate given the scale of this young man's criminality. Therefore, the probation officer decided that a custodial sentence was the only appropriate thing to recommend. It would be a punishment for the youth's planned, continuous and large-scale criminal activities, but the probation service would be able to offer through-care and after-care facilities. However, there would be few positive elements about such a sentence for a young man with a previous good record of behaviour. Ultimately, the probation officer acknowledged that the court would inevitably make a custodial sentence.

Goal-setting

In this case, the goal seemed to be an acknowledgment of a custodial sentence, whilst demonstrating an awareness of risk and need. Even so, goals were set in the recommendation for custody: to establish stable work patterns, to accept the guidance of a male authority figure and to make the resources of the probation service available during through-care and after-care. The goals lay in making an assessment, communicating this to the court and the offender and preparing for through-care work. However, the officer was faced with a dilemma. He knew that it was almost inevitable that the youth would be given a custodial sentence but the officer wanted the court to make this decision; he did not want to say it would be a good thing and so feel that the initiative for the sentence was his rather than the court's. Therefore at the final hurdle, the officer opted out and did not make a specific recommendation for either borstal training or imprisonment as a young person. The court sentenced the youth to borstal training.

Assessment/intervention

There were two interesting things about the stages of the social work process in this case. First, a new assessment had to be made whilst intervention through the probation order was in progress. This meant that there was some blurring and telescoping of the acquisition and study stages of the assessment, because the probation officer had already studied aspects of the offender's environment before he began to acquire information for the new inquiry. The officer knew that he had to gather information for the new inquiry in a very specific way. Second, the need for intervention may involve other agencies besides the probation service, so, as he was assessing, this officer had to anticipate the various resources which could be mobilised in future through the penal system and the probation service. The intervention which had been done through the existing probation order had influenced the officer's assessment, because for various reasons, that type of supervision seemed to have had no impact on the youth's criminality.

Great skill is needed when goals are being set in assessments which indicate the appropriateness of institutional facilities. However much the phases of the assessment process are telescoped, or the stages of assessment and intervention overlap, it is important to keep the purpose of the inquiry in clear focus and to be clear about the facilities and options available.

6 Inappropriateness of an institutional sentence indicated

One of the historical functions of the probation service has been to keep offenders out of prison, so it is not surprising that officers are often involved in making efforts to keep people out of custody. They usually have specific reasons for setting such goals: the offender will either be damaged or not helped by being imprisoned; such a sentence would have personal and social repercussions on the family; the offender has responded well to supervision even though he has committed further offences, and he is motivated to change his behaviour; medical and psychiatric rather than custodial treatment is indicated; the situation has changed so much that there is little risk of further offences; the need for help is overwhelming; a custodial sentence would meet the court's requirements for retribution, deterrence and punishment, but would damage the offender. A variety of recommendations can be made as a means of keeping offenders out of prison, depending on the risk, need and resources balance sheet: conditional discharge, fine, probation, suspended sentence with or without supervision, community service order and deferred sentences. Probation officers will, therefore, set goals in their social inquiry reports which will either argue against a custodial sentence or present an assessment which will try to ensure that an institutional measure is not given.

For example,* a juvenile offender, aged fifteen, who was already on supervision to a probation officer was charged with assault and a further social inquiry report was prepared. He had been subject to a supervision order following an offence on a police officer during a dispute in his home, and he had been to an attendance centre after being convicted of a theft offence. The probation officer had seen the boy on his own in the office, with his family at home, and in a group during an intermediate treatment programme. The first news of a possible further court appearance came from the boy when he obliquely mentioned to the officer that the police were inquiring about an accident when he had hit another boy at school. Notice of the forthcoming court appearance came subsequently from the boy's headmaster and the juvenile bureau.

The boy lived with his mother and two younger siblings; the father was separated from his wife, but regularly visited the children at home.

Acquisition

The officer had a lot of recent and current information about the boy and his relationships with his family and in his social environment. He also had access to old agency records relating to the father's previous contact with the probation service. The main sources of information throughout the current inquiry were the boy, his parents, the school, and the social services department to whom the mother had appealed for help with the boy. The officer had to keep the purpose and focus of his inquiry on the current offence, even though he was able to set this against the backcloth of the many things he knew about the boy and his circumstances. The officer's

*The social inquiry report which was presented in this case is outlined in Appendix II/D.

reactions to the news of the offence were interesting, as he explained, 'I thought, "he has done it at last". There was a lot of aggression in his general behaviour and mannerisms and in all my contacts with him, even though the aggression was latent rather than overt'. The officer realised that communication would be difficult with this boy. Because the boy was known, the interviews were more loosely structured than they would have been if he had been working on a new inquiry. The boy was withdrawn and non-communicative, which the officer thought was related to his bottling up a lot of things inside him and not wanting to let anything out at all. This was not just a normal adolescent inability to talk to an adult, and the officer found it difficult to share his assessment with the youth. An interview was specifically set up to discuss the offence and forthcoming court appearance and it took place, 'half over a game of table tennis . . . a shallow interview which was basically fact-finding and not much to do with feelings. . . . It was in that interview he mentioned that the boy whom he had hit said something about him not having a father'. Communication with the mother was easier in one sense because she talked easily, but the officer had to help her to focus on the offence and the inquiry rather than on all her other difficulties. Contact was not made with the father at this point, partly because he was working away from home, but also as he had negative views about probation officers resulting from his own criminal history. Information was sought from the school and from the social worker who knew the family. However, as the boy was the focus of the inquiry, it was communication blocks with him which had to be overcome.

Study

The officer was aware that he knew more than was necessary for the inquiry, but the framework for study still had to be related to the offence, the offender and the court. The offence was considered in an individualised way rather than on the tariff, because it was thought to be an expression of the boy's frustration and aggression which had been referred to by his family and teachers. Strengths and stresses in the boy's situation were carefully studied. There were stresses in the home situation because the mother could not cope and had asked for the boy to be received into care; the boy had had problems in the school from which he had been suspended and his teachers were asking for him to go into care; the boy was also facing delinquent pressures from his peers. However, the one strength in the situation was that the father had suggested that the boy should move to live with him once his new home was ready. Whilst the boy minimised the offence by claiming that he hit out in self-defence, the probation officer saw his behaviour as a reflection of recent family difficulties and thought that it was a continuation of the aggression he was displaying in other situations, including the intermediate treatment group. The officer knew that the court would take a serious view of the offence, but probation resources were still available for him, so it was important to ensure that the right decision was made in court.

Formulation

The process of weighing up the risks, needs and resources was a continuing theme throughout the inquiry because of the amount of information the officer already had. Risk and need were assessed in very precise ways. Risk was measured by using Davies's *Index of the Social Environment* (1973). This boy scored the maximum on every factor: crime contamination because he had previous convictions, delinquent friends and a father with a criminal history; support in the mother's home was nil and the father had previously offered little support; his school was a negative experience. The high risk arose from the boy's situation rather than from the actual seriousness of his criminal offences. Need was measured using Heimler's (1975) social scale, which indicated that the boy was in need of institutional support. The officer also estimated the boy's needs as high because he had many problems and required help. Resources were available in the probation agency, the boy was already a member of an intermediate treatment group, and the officer was concerned about him and wanted to continue with the supervision order. A means had to be found to allow the boy to continue with social work help and to move to his father's home. These could not be achieved if a care order was made or the boy was sent to a detention centre. The supervision order had another two years to run; this order also contained an intermediate treatment measure and the boy was also reporting to an attendance centre.

Goal-setting

The main goal set at this inquiry was to ensure that social work intervention through the probation order was continued, so that the probation officer could carry on with the work he was already doing and the boy could go to live with his father. The probation officer set an additional goal, because he wanted the court to make some gesture of disapproval towards the boy about his aggressive behaviour. The officer shared his thinking with the boy, and told him that he agreed that he should go to live with his father. He indicated that he did not condone the boy's behaviour, but it was difficult to make a meaningful contractual agreement in this situation. The officer and the boy each agreed that it was a good idea for him to go and live with his father and that they would try to bring this about; whilst the boy wanted this, *his* main concern was to avoid going to a detention centre. The financial penalty which was recommended, was a means of giving expression to these two goals; it would enable supervision to continue and it would register a disapproval about the boy's behaviour.

Assessment/intervention

The probation officer had to be very clear about the two roles he was playing with this boy. On the one hand he was working with the boy and his family and school through the supervision order and intermediate treatment group. On the other hand, he was making an assessment for a social inquiry in relation to a new offence. His intervention could have distorted his assessment in two different ways. First, the officer could have become so involved in and identified with the boy that he made a faulty assessment of the boy's capacity and motivation for change and underestimated the seriousness of the offence. Second, the officer could have used his existing knowledge of the case to distort the nature of the current offence. The officer was obviously using a 'treatment model' explanation of the boy's current delinquency, because he saw the assault offence in relation to the juvenile's background and as a symptom of his difficulties. The officer acknowledged the seriousness of the assault but did not accept the boy's justification of self-defence, and he did not think it was a case of a freely-chosen and isolated infraction. It can only be speculated that a different view might have been taken of the offence had the officer not been working with the offender and his family. There are many dilemmas in juvenile justice, especially if one process is violated when an offender is sentenced on the basis of a treatment model rather than the tariff (Bean, 1976; Bottoms, 1974; Lemert, 1976; Matza, 1964; May, 1971). This boy had originally become subject to supervision because of his needs rather than the gravity of his offence and criminal history. By the time he appeared in court for the third time, he was due for detention centre on a straight tariff. The probation officer could have either gone along with this, or even recommended a detention centre on grounds of need, had not the father stepped in at the crucial moment with his offer of a home. The probation officer was very clear about the purpose of his assessment for the inquiry; because of his previous and current intervention, he was able to find a balance between a tariff and a treatment measure, so that alternatives to an institutional sentence were considered. He was well aware of the ethical issues involved. Some writers argue that there are so many problems raised by the use of treatment models in juvenile justice cases that social workers should opt for pure tariff measures even at the expense of some people's needs. This goes to the heart of theory and practice in social work, because justice requires that some people are given some individual consideration (Aubert, 1963, p. 201; Taylor, *et al.*, 1973). The case just described illustrates some of these dilemmas.

The sentence is the goal

There are two senses in which the actual sentence may be the goal in social inquiry situations. First, the assessment, intervention and evaluation stages of the social work process are sometimes telescoped during the inquiry stage because crisis work has been done or immediate needs have been met. A conditional discharge or small fine is sometimes recommended as a symbolic gesture in these circumstances. Secondly an actual sentence can be thought of as a treatment measure. For example, a conditional discharge is recommended because an offender needs to have the 'courts's continuing presence' as a background to her life. In other situations, people are positively helped by having to pay a fine because they accept that their criminal behaviour was wrong and want to clear their conscience and recompense society.

Situations in which goals are not set

Probation officers do not always set goals as they complete their social inquiry with an offender (Hardiker, 1975, 1977b). This may occur (though it need not) if the inevitability of a custodial sentence is acknowledged because either the offender is a professional criminal who has taken calculated risks and does not want help, or he is a recidivist for whom social work intervention is inappropriate. When probation officers do not set goals, they frequently do not make a recommendation to the court. This may be because they cannot bring themselves to recommend custody or they see no point in commenting on the inevitability of imprisonment. Sometimes, probation officers think that their main function in social inquiries is to assess the need for probation (The Morison Report, 1962), and, if this is not indicated, they leave the court to decide on other measures. Another reason why probation officers do not make a recommendation is that the offender is seen to be a client for psychiatric rather than social work help and the sentence is left to medical opinion. The officer may also opt out of setting goals and making a recommendation when legal issues such as not guilty pleas are at stake. Occasionally, the officer may feel that his inquiry had not produced enough data for him to go through the formulation process adequately; in these circumstances he either does not make a recommendation, or asks for a further adjournment. Finally, the omission of a recommendation may mean that, though the officer has views about a choice of disposal, he is not prepared to negotiate it directly through his report. He might express his views at the court hearing if asked, or he might abdicate his responsibility for the client to the sentencer's decision. In these situations, goal-setting is not taken to its logical conclusion.

We have described a number of circumstances in which probation officers set goals in relation to different types and agencies of intervention in their social inquiry work. In some cases, there is no question about the need for or appropriateness of intervention. In other situations, the need for help is evident, but it can be provided more appropriately by other agencies than the probation service. When intervention seems to be indicated, the court needs to know whether this should be provided in the community or within an institution. Though probation officers sometimes opt out of their goal-setting function by making no recommendation, they usually give expression to their goals by suggesting a particular sentence. As we have seen, the same recommendation can be made for a variety of reasons, and similar goals may be achieved through a wide range of sentencing disposals.

Goal-setting in social inquiries has been described in terms of recommendations which may indicate whether or not some kind of intervention is needed. Whilst this is the essence of goal-setting activities at this stage, probation officers sometimes anticipate more specific intervention goals in their social inquiries. For example, they may suggest to the court that supervision may assist with family conflicts, or provide an entry into group activities, or offer support and assistance to an offender. It is perfectly appropriate for probation officers to anticipate and mention such intervention goals, even though they will probably be renegotiated after the court hearing. Even so, it is important to recognise the limits and boundaries of goal-setting at the social inquiry/assessment stage of the social work process.

Contracting in social inquiries

We have referred previously to the importance of sharing information with clients throughout the different stages of the assessment process. This seems to be essential so that worker and client can jointly negotiate their plans. But any agreement made at this stage should be primarily in relation to the recommendation for the court rather than to long-term intervention plans which the sentencers might authorise. For example, if the worker is discussing with the client the possibility of probation supervision, he has a responsibility to explain what he means by such an intervention for that particular client and to make explicit what his expectations will be. He should specify the objectives and share his ideas for the plan of intervention to achieve those aims in relation to the problem. Then the client can indicate whether he agrees with either the problems as identified or the means whereby supervision would alleviate them. Thus, the contract can be discussed, negotiated and agreed before the court hearing, but it should not be implemented until the court has authorised the means whereby it can take effect.

Contracting does not imply that there is total agreement between the worker and client. As Sainsbury (1970) points out, it is necessary to distinguish between the worker's professional opinion and the client's parallel and related appraisal of the situation. The worker's definition of the problem will derive from his practice theories, which are based on scientific knowledge, an awareness of stresses in the client's life, values, feelings and some assessment about the client's motivation. Even so, the worker should share his assessment with the client so that the latter's views can be sought. In 'custody inevitable' inquiries, the offender may agree to differ with the probation officer but the outcome of the assessment should still be shared with him. Sometimes, the options available become part of the assessment so that contracting can go on way before the report is presented in court. Workers cannot always assume that there is a probation order coming and plan for it beforehand, so they may have to discuss with the client various plans to help him and his family if he is sent to prison.

The idea of contracting may be even more complex when the inquiry is undertaken by an intake worker, and the subsequent intervention is taken over by a colleague in the long-term treatment teams. This may avoid the pitfall of implementing the contract precipitously, but there may be a danger in leaving the agreement too uncertain and vague so that the client feels surprised at the commitment he is expected to give, or disappointed at the level of help he is being offered. Even when the assessment and transfer are done well, it may be necessary to revise the assessment when the intervention begins.

Contract theory is still in its infancy in social work (Hutton, 1977; Maluccio and Marlow, 1974), particularly in relation to social inquiry work. At this stage in our knowledge it is probably safer to think of contracts in the loose sense of agreements between social workers and clients. Whatever form the agreement takes, it should be shared with the client, be specific about commitment, objectives and means of achieving these, and be made in the full knowledge that the sentencers (or equivalent) are a party to the contract.

Use of reports

Throughout this book we have discussed social inquiries, but it seems pertinent to refer briefly to the report for the court. The Streatfeild Report (1961) indicated the boundaries of relevance and competence in social inquiry reports, but developments in training and practice have subsequently occurred, alongside changes in the expectations of courts and probation officers. Other writers (Mathieson and Walker, 1971; Perry, 1974; Mathieson and Herbert, 1975) have identified some of the skills involved in writing social inquiry reports, so we shall confine our comments to practice theories in these documents.

First, the report is a document for the court rather than a casework plan. It should include the probation officer's assessment of the situation and this will include some specification of the goals which have been set during the inquiry. The structure and content of the report should support the goals outlined in the conclusion and recommendation. The document may be a pointer to the work that is planned, but it should not include the social work hypotheses, explorations and prognoses. The principle underlying the report is that it is a document with which to advise sentencers and to negotiate in the court.

Second, once the principles and purposes behind reports are clear to the worker, there are particular skills involved in communicating the assessment. The report should be readily understood by other professionals such as lawyers, informed laymen (magistrates) and the offender. It should be free from social work jargon and distinguish between verified fact and opinion. If the worker feels uncertain about some of his information, he should indicate this, but be confident about his professional opinion which is supported by social work skill, knowledge and values.

Third, a worker's practice theories will affect the way in which he filters and selects his information for the court. This means that he will have particular reasons for omitting and including particular types of data, or playing up and playing down certain indicators of strength and stresses (Hardiker, 1975; 1977b). The worker's principles of practice, based on the skills, knowledge and values of his profession, should ensure that he presents a picture that is fair to the client and appropriate for the court's purposes. This remains a problematical issue, because some people argue (Hardiker, 1978) that the probation officer should openly present the reasons for his assessment if he is secure in his professional competence and role in relation to sentencers. However, some social workers believe that social inquiry reports are 'moral' documents, which are presented as a kind of defence for the client.

Fourth, it is important to specify the roles which probation officers play as they present their reports, because the contents of the documents will vary accordingly (Hardiker, 1977b; 1978). In most cases probation officers advise sentencers, and in these circumstances their reports present either a relatively straightforward description of the offender's circumstances or a diagnosis and prognosis of his criminal behaviour. However, in some cases, probation officers play a more strategic role because they try to manipulate the sentencers towards making a 'social work' decision, and this often occurs when attempts are made to keep offenders out of prison. In these circumstances, an offender's response to supervision may be played up and his life difficulties either played down or omitted. There are some situations in which officers play a classical justice role in their court reports by acknowledging the inevitability of a tariff sentence. Their court reports may then either play up an offender's incorrigibility and life stresses or omit mitigating evidence. The main point which is being made here is that the probation officer must be clear about his principles and practice as he plays these different roles, because the context of his social inquiry report are a logical outcome of these. There is some evidence about the circumstances in which these different roles are played (*ibid.*), and this is not the place to evaluate them. The issue is problematical and has profound implications for the structure and content of social inquiry reports.

Some of the goal-setting illustrations presented in this chapter illustrate the ways in which sentencing roles shape the content of the social inquiry report. In the probation high need case (4), where social work intervention was indicated, the officer informed the court through his report all that he could about the offender's circumstances to justify his goal of probation supervision. He was playing a straightforward, advising-sentencers role. In case 6, where the inappropriateness of an institutional sentence was indicated, the probation officer presented the court with information that pointed to the boy being given the chance to live with his father; less was said about the potential difficulties related to some of the boy's problematic behaviour with his peers in the intermediate treatment group. In this sense, the probation officer was shaping the contents of his report in order to influence the sentencers towards a 'social work decision'. In case 5, the probation officer ultimately opted for a classical justice rôle, because he acknowledged the inevitability of a custodial sentence given the seriousness of the offences. We can speculate that he might have played up the peculiar features of the youth's early life, the current stresses he was facing, and his response to supervision, if an attempt had been made to keep the offender out of prison. In terms of the probation officers' goals and the roles they chose to play, the information presented in their reports was relevant and comprehensive.

Practice theories

These probation officers were engaged in a complex filtering process as they set goals with the offenders in their social inquiry work. There was evidence that the officers were drawing on some explicit theories of practice in order to make sense of, and reach an assessment in their work. For example, in the conditional discharge case (2) involving a domestic assault, the officer was drawing on his knowledge about cultural and social norms in order to see the offence in a meaningful context. In the probation case (4), the officer was using his knowledge about crisis intervention and the ways in which previous experiences and current stresses can affect the functioning of young adults at the beginning stages of their marriage. In the case where the inevitability of a custodial sentence was acknowledged (5), the officer's work was informed by his psychological and sociological knowledge; he carefully examined the early background of the client and the ways in which it did not automatically influence the youth's current functioning; the critical stage of development which the youth had reached was also recognised, especially given the need for guidance and in the absence of a male authority figure on which to model behaviour; this knowledge of personal development was also examined in the context of the youth's cultural, class and community background because the offences seemed to be related to drift within a delinquent subculture. In case 6, the worker drew on his knowledge about adolescence, family interaction and community networks. In none of these cases did the officers strictly adhere to one or more theoretical stance because they had to rely on other knowledge besides their explicit theories.

For example, each of the workers had some 'practice wisdom' about their own agency's function in relation to other resources in the community. The officer in the conditional discharge case (2) placed expertise for child care in the social services department but would have accepted responsibility to intervene if a difficult marital problem had been presented. In the probation case (4), the officer was able to do crisis work not just because he knew about the theory and method but also because he combined this with his knowledge of community resources and his skills in working with other agencies. The worker with the adolescent (6) was working with the school and intermediate treatment group as he assessed the boy's potential, and he used particular scales (Heinler, 1975) to help him in his task.

The workers were also relying on their feelings and observations about the offenders on whom they were making an inquiry. In the conditional discharge case (2), the officer observed the family's home conditions and life style, but felt that there were strengths in the situation for the people involved—the worker would not have wanted to live in such conditions himself. It was apparent that the officer identified with the offenders in their distress in the probation case (4); he was prepared to reach out to each of them whilst keeping clear about his role in relation to them. In the custody-inevitable case (5), the officer blended his theoretical knowledge with his practice experience, because he had to make sense of a multitude of facts, theories, feelings and observations about the situation in relation to that particular youth; it was not enough for him just to assess that the youth had had problems in his childhood and currently lived in a delinquent area; such knowledge had to be telescoped in relation to the unique constellation of life experiences of the youth at that particular time. Whatever theories the officer had about the adolescent (6), he had to try to communicate with the boy about his current situation and future prospects. Social workers have to carry around in their heads a combination of thoughts, feelings and observations about complex situations and actively to use these various sources of knowledge in a unique blend in order to make sense of each individual case.

The final word must be kept for John Smith's probation officer. He set the goal of social work help through probation supervision so as to give guidance and support to John Smith at a difficult time and so that he would not attempt to solve his problems by criminal means. The officer was engaged in an active process of conceptualisation as he filtered a mass of data in this case. As he acquired his information, he was observing the man in his family and had some feelings about how far he was responsible for his criminal activities. The officer was also drawing on psycho-dynamic frameworks as he studied the case; he individualised the offences in relation to the man's feelings of rejection, insecurity and loss of masculine pride. There seemed to be more stresses than strengths in the situation, and social control systems could be mobilised appropriately. A treatment ideology helped the officer to make sense of this case, because the offences were analysed in relation to the offender's background and were seen as symptom of the need for social work intervention. All these thoughts, feelings and observations were used in the formulation, in which the high need and moderate high risk in the situation seemed to be manageable through the use of probation resources. Therefore, as the probation officer was making his assessment, he was applying theory. But his practice theories rested on other things besides an explicit psycho-dynamic theory of practice. The officer had to rely on other sources of knowledge and his own feelings and perceptions in order to make sense of the case. The process of using knowledge and the ability to integrate this in order to come to some conclusion in a particular case are the essence of practice theories. The officer's conclusion was informed by his understanding that a man whose early history of deprivation and rejection and current problems of ill health and unemployment might be redressed and compensated by being offered opportunites of support and dependence on a professional worker. He showed understanding also of the importance of increasing a client's self-esteem in order to help him to function more competently in his roles of husband and father.

Chapter six

Assessment processes in different social work settings

In the preceding chapters we utilised material obtained from a research sample of ninety probation inquiries, in order to examine the relevance of our assessment model. In this chapter we shall explore the relevance of the model to inquiries in other social work settings.

Part I consists of an account of assessment processes in three different social work settings, namely, a local authority social services department area team, a child treatment research unit, and a hospital-based social work team.

In Part II we present an analysis of these three cases, using the assessment framework used in the previous chapters. We shall explore the interpersonal process which took place in the communication between workers and clients. The frameworks with which the workers studied the information which was obtained will then be examined. Some comparisons will be made between the assessments which were formulated, as each worker weighed up risks, needs and resources. Finally, we shall consider the processes by which goals were identified at the end of the assessment stage in each case. Interwoven in the analysis will be some consideration of the distinct phases of assessment and intervention and the social workers' practice theories.

The analysis of these three cases provides illustrative evidence that the model which was applied to the probation inquiries can be generalised to all social work situations, even though the content and boundaries of the work undertaken differed.

Part I Three social work assessments

Method of obtaining material

Three social workers each agreed to select a case which could be discussed with us. The case should illustrate their activities in a piece of assessment work but apart from this the workers were free to choose any type of social work situation. The agency base of each of the three workers has already been indicated in the introduction.

The social workers sent us brief details of the selected cases. An interview schedule for each case was prepared. (See Appendix I for the one used in the case of the non-accidental injury. In the other two cases a similar schedule, appropriately modified, was used). A tape-recorded, focused interview was then conducted with each of the workers. In the Child Treatment Research Unit the director of the unit was the social worker but had worked on this inquiry with a less experienced worker and both were interviewed. The transcripts of these interviews formed the basis for the narratives which follow.

We have chosen to present the three accounts of assessment activities in order of the age of the client on whom the referral was focused.

Case A An inquiry into a non-accidental injury to a baby

Background

Miss Bell, a senior social worker in a social services department intake team took a referral from the emergency duty officer: a query non-accidental injury to a four-and-a-half-week-old baby. The duty officer noted, 'Mr and Mrs Jones called out the emergency duty doctor last night because they "suddenly noticed bruises on him as they were bathing him" '. The baby was admitted to hospital, where the parents were willing to leave him.

The social services department had a statutory obligation to intervene under the 1969 Children and Young Persons Act, Part I. Section 1 (2) (a) of the act covers cases where the child's proper development is being avoidably prevented or neglected, or his health is being avoidably impaired or neglected, or he is being ill-treated.

Acquisition of information

Miss Bell had to complete a thorough assessment within ten days for a case conference, when a decision would be made about future intervention. She contacted and interviewed numerous people in order to gather relevant information for her assessment.

The referral note contained basic information about the injury, the age of the baby and his parents, their address and the family composition.

(a) the baby had two bruises, one on the right thigh and one on the left leg plus a scratch over his eyes. He seemed otherwise well nourished and cared for.

(b) Mr and Mrs Jones lived with Mr Jones's parents and there

were believed to be other people in the house. Mr Jones was employed and there were no other children of the marriage.
(c) The doctor said the parents were willing to see a social worker.
(d) Mr Jones was twenty-one and Mrs Jones was eighteen.

Miss Bell telephoned the doctor at the hospital, who provided the same information as had been given in the referral note.

She telephoned the child abuse centre in the area to check whether the baby was on the at risk register, which he was not. She then contacted the doctor who was the specialist in community medicine to ask her to visit the child at the hospital with the social worker.

Miss Bell telephoned the family doctor to find out who was the health visitor. This health visitor described her visits to the home and the baby's attendance at the clinic. She also provided information about the home circumstances, thought the house was reasonable for the area and that there was a good standard of hygiene and homecraft within it with plenty of advice and encouragement to the mother. The baby seemed all right.

Miss Bell telephoned the emergency doctor who had gone out to see the child. When he turned up at the house, the grandmother, parents and baby were there and the baby was sitting on the grandmother's knee. They said that they had noticed the bruising when they bathed the baby and that they felt it was spontaneous bruising; 'it had been coming on since the morning'. They said they called the emergency doctor out because they were frightened. The doctor examined the baby and admitted him to hospital because of the nature of the bruising. The family agreed to this. They thought, if it was a blood disorder, the sooner it was checked the better. The doctor also said that when he walked into the house, 'you could have cut the air with a knife', and he wondered if there had been a row about the baby.

Miss Bell wrote down some warning signs:

(a) The delay in seeking medical advice
(b) The emergency doctor rather than the GP had been called
(c) Bruises could not have been self-inflicted by a four-and-a-half-week-old baby
(d) Was there stress from the home situation—how overcrowded was the house and what were relationships like? Why did the parents not have their own home? Was there interference from the mother-in-law, and did the teenage children resent having a 'bawling brat' around the house? What were the sleeping arrangements? Did the parents have to try and keep the baby quiet?

The social worker asked the records clerk if the family was known to the social services department. Later on it was found that the mother had been in trouble for minor offences during her adolescence.

Miss Bell saw the baby at the hospital, at first on her own, and then with the community physician. He looked a very well-nourished baby and was asleep but looked perfectly normal. He was reported to be quite lively and responsive when awake. He had bruising on the outside of one thigh and around the knee area of the other leg. The social worker and the doctor compared their observations and talked about how the bruising might have happened. The social worker then discussed the case with the hospital staff and said that she was not happy about the situation, and neither were they. The staff told her that the parents' explanation had been about the baby perhaps having something wrong with his blood. The staff also said that the child was placid, well-nourished, a normally developed baby with no feeding problems. They also commented that the bruises could not possibly have been self-inflicted.

Miss Bell interviewed the parents at the hospital by prior arrangement. They were both nervous and the mother seemed agitated. The worker explained her involvement to them very carefully, using some of the cases that had been in the news and explaining why things had gone wrong as illustrations; she described her department's procedures and told the parents of their legal rights. She encouraged them to get a solicitor after the case conference if the case was going to court. She explained what a place of safety order meant and what would happen next.

The parents could offer no explanation of how the bruising had occurred. They kept coming back to the idea that the child must have something wrong with his blood because the mother's family had got something wrong with their blood and she had this condition when she was younger. At that stage, the social worker had received the results of the first blood test which indicated that the blood was perfectly normal.

Miss Bell asked the parents to explain how it had happened that the baby had got into hospital; the mother told her that she had not noticed the bruising earlier in the day or when she had been changing the baby after his two o'clock feed. During the evening they thought they noticed blood on the baby's shawl. They had a look at him and it proved not to be blood but on checking him over discovered the bruising on his legs. Rather than wait until the following day for the surgery, they thought they should seek medical advice immediately.

The next day the results of the blood tests were known definitely. The second sample showed that the child had no medical condition which could have caused the bruising. The skeletal survey had also shown no previous fractures.

Miss Bell went to the hospital and saw the mother who was visiting the child. She told her the results of the blood test and that this meant that either the child had had an accident or that someone had got cross and smacked him; in view of his age and vulnerability and their lack of knowledge on which to base a decision about what should be done for the best, she was definitely going to apply to the court for a place of safety order. Miss Bell had taken another social worker with her, partly for the experience but also because she had dealt with it all the previous day and felt in need of support.

The mother cried for quite a long time. She was asked where the father would be. As he would be at home at lunch-time, they went there to tell him what was happening. The father was upset but made no objection to the arrangements. The grandparents were also very upset and very aggressive at first. The social worker interviewed first the parents alone in the kitchen, then the grandparents in the living room, and explained to each couple in turn how the situation appeared to her:

> At this stage nobody is prepared to tell me what has happened but, whatever the explanation is, I am left with a baby of four weeks old with quite serious bruising, with nobody prepared to tell me how it had happened. So I have no way of knowing whether I can prevent it happening again.

The social worker told them that she had no choice about what to do, held on to that, but went through her story several times. The family calmed down in the end and accepted it: they became quite co-operative for a while.

At that point, Miss Bell applied for a place of safety order from the magistrates' court. The child remained in hospital for another five days and the parents were prepared to accept that. They could visit him freely, and the social worker and the ward staff encouraged them to do so.

Miss Bell began to arrange foster-care for the baby. The foster-mother was away on holiday, so she bargained with the hospital to keep the baby for a few more days. Then five days later—after the bank holiday—she called on the parents and took them down to the hospital to pick up the baby and they all visited the foster-home. Prior to this visit, the social worker had explained to the foster-mother what her expectations were of both the foster parents and the parents. Arrangements were agreed.

When they turned up at the foster-home, the discussion was more difficult than had been anticipated because only the foster-mother's mother was there (the foster-mother had been delayed in returning from her holiday) and the older woman then said all the wrong things. She described how they had had a foster-child whom they later adopted. Miss Bell had spent a lot of time explaining to the baby's parents that fostering and adoption were not the same thing, to try to allay their fears about losing the baby. When the foster-mother arrived, introductions were made and arrangements planned for the parents to visit the baby the next day.

The child had been put into the foster-home for basic care and also to enable the social worker to assess the parent-child interaction and continue with the overall task of assessing the context in which the non-accidental injury had taken place.

Miss Bell visited the maternal grandmother at her home. Prior to this visit, she had found out more about the history of this family from the health visitor. The baby's maternal uncle lived on the same estate, was married with three children who were all on the 'at risk' register; two of them had sustained quite serious injuries. The worker had also met the maternal grandparents at the hospital on the day that the baby had been moved to the foster home. The grandmother had been quite aggressive that day, understandably so because she did not know what was going on. She had been to the hospital having heard that the hospital would not let the baby go, saying that she wanted him and then finding out the story about the bruising and social services involvement. Then when the social worker talked things through, the maternal grandmother calmed down quite quickly, and she expressed some concern about the relationship between the baby's parents.

The maternal grandmother told the social worker that she was, 'totally shocked by the whole thing and nothing like this had ever happened in her family before'. (The health visitor had told the social worker that it was this mother who had covered up for her son in the previous cases of child abuse).

Throughout this period, Miss Bell kept in regular touch with the baby's parents, she acquired a lot of information from a variety of people. She had several interviews with the baby's parents and both sets of grandparents, at their home and in the hospital. She also contacted the health visitor, doctors, foster-parents and her own colleagues. In the process she was gaining new information, but also checking and re-checking stories from different sources.

Studying facts and feelings

This case involved a complex process of study for Miss Bell. She was trying to make sense of the facts she was gathering but she was also hypothesising about some of them and trying to test out the validity of her hypotheses. We shall first describe how she studied her early information and then what story the total picture seemed to convey to her.

Picking up clues

When Miss Bell first took the referral—query non-accidental injury —the address told her something: 'It is an established council estate on which we have a great many clients. It is fairly vandalised, low level housing, and there is a lot of unemployment and delinquency there'. When she found out the age of the parents, this also conveyed something to her:

It tells me that they are very young people. Was she pregnant before she was married? If they are living with in-laws the like-lihood is that it was not a planned pregnancy, so I wonder how much they wanted this baby and about how they and the rest of the family feel about it.

Miss Bell speculated that there might be family stress, but she held back on that until she went to see the family: 'I did not know exactly what the house was like. I did not know the road in question well enough to be able to tell exactly the whereabouts of the house; there is a variety of council housing on that road'.

Miss Bell began her search for explanations of the bruising:

If the parents have given an explanation of the bruising and give you, or anyone else who is involved, an explanation, then it is significant if they do not tie up. It may mean that they have changed the story because they can see the look of unbelief on people's faces. It may also mean that they are covering some-thing up because they cannot face telling people what has really happened.

The social worker checked the story from the hospital doctor. She followed up clues about the family through the health visitor, who thought the baby and the family were coping all right, but also described the circumstances of the family.

Then Miss Bell obtained one story of the bruising from the emergency doctor: 'They had noticed the bruising when they bathed the baby and they felt it was spontaneous bruising—it had been coming on since the morning'. Miss Bell studied the information she had alongside her own observations of the baby at the hospital:

I put my hands in various positions to see how these bruises might have been caused. One explanation which I was very likely to get from the parents was that he had fallen off some-thing but there is no way in which a baby of four weeks is

107

going to be able to fall of something and bruise the outside of both legs. It would be either one side or the other. I wanted to be fairly sure myself of how I felt it had happened, so that I could talk about what the reality of the bruising was when they were telling me their tale of how it had happened. The doctor and I then wondered whether it was somebody with a very large hand, left-handed, or whether it was a slap on both sides of the thighs. There was a very faint bruise on his forehead, but it had faded and that kind of information would not have been acceptable to the court. So we are left with two quite extensive bruises on the legs.

At this stage, the hospital repeated the parents' story about the baby having something wrong with his blood.

In her interviews with the parents Miss Bell picked up more clues about them:

The parents looked less bright and healthy than I had expected. They were not angry and I was very worried about this. I got absolutely no negative feelings back from them. The mother cried a lot during the interview, and at one stage when she was crying quite bitterly I had put my arms around her. She put her arms round my neck and absolutely clung to me and would not let go of me. I was quite shocked by that. I thought, 'whatever has this girl got in life if she has to use me who has done something so awful to her—or does she see it as being awful; maybe she does not'.

The parents could not offer an explanation at all of how the bruising had occurred. They kept coming back to the story about his blood. Then, when they told her that they had not noticed the bruising earlier in the day or when she had changed the nappy at two o'clock, the social worker noticed the discrepancy between that story and the one they had given the doctor. They had told the latter that, 'it had been coming on since morning'. Then when the parents talked about the blood on the shawl, the social worker wondered what that meant:

I looked at it in one of two ways. Either, they contacted the emergency doctor very quickly and they did the right thing— but what was the blood they thought they saw? Or, were they afraid? Is that what they would have liked to have done to the baby, or is it what they were afraid they might have done to the baby?

At this stage Miss Bell felt that she, 'knew already that somebody had hit the baby'.

The question now was, how important is it to find out
exactly who did it? It may be important in terms of justice to
find out exactly who did it. It may be important in terms of
preventing it happening again, which is the primary thing. On
the other hand you may do more harm than good by pushing it
too hard. You are not there as a detective. I am there as a
social worker and the roles are a bit different. If they are not
going to tell me who did it, if they know, then how important
is it going to be. I was playing around with ideas like that.

After the social worker had seen the baby's parents, she then
studied the grandparents' story.

Both grandparents said very definitely that there was no way
the mother would have done it, she loved the baby. Neither
would the father have done it—nobody would have hit him.
There were other possibilities. His mother had taken him down
to her sister's and that was a rough household. I was beginning
to get the picture that the two families did not like each other
and did not get on.

Miss Bell studied the parents' handling of the baby:

The father had the fairly typical reaction of it being a very
small baby and was not too happy about holding him very
much. He seemed to think he would break if he held him too
tightly. The mother was adept with him; I was surprised because he was very tiny and floppy and she managed him very
well and deftly. She had had quite a lot of experience with tiny
babies such as her sisters'.

Miss Bell moved to speculation about the bonding processes:

There was nothing to break the bonding as far as I could see.
The mother had not gone to work, it had not been an abnormal
birth and there had been no separation afterwards. She looked
at him when she fed him and there was eye contact. She
handled him as though he was fairly precious, so I felt bonding
had happened.

The social worker wanted to study the interactions more closely,
and thought that a fostering situation would enable the bonding
between the mother and the baby to be observed properly. She also
wanted the mother to feel that she could build up some trust with the
foster-mother: 'This is often a problem when children come into
care; there is a great fear on the parents' part that the foster-mother
is going to take over, particularly with a small baby'. Miss Bell
wanted the father to be involved as well, though she realised that she

was imposing her own values and views about sex roles on the parents.

Miss Bell then re-examined the issue about responsibility for the bruising. She eventually decided that her priority was to understand the context in which the incident had taken place.

> In this case I had the nasty feeling that we would never find out who did it, and we never did, although I am fairly sure I know now. But I have never known for sure who did it. In fact I do not think it has ever been that important.
>
> What was more important was to try and find out more about the background of these young and vulnerable parents with such a messy looking extended family. My job was to try to predict the likelihood of it happening again and whether there were variables that we could change that would make that less likely.

So Miss Bell studied her role in quite a complex way. At one level the bruising could be seen as perhaps the presenting symptom of underlying problems. At another level, if the baby had stayed at home, the next thing might have been a more serious or even a fatal injury if nobody had grasped what the problem was and intervened: 'My feeling was there were other problems in the family and this is how these problems had come to light, but I am not saying they deliberately did it so that these problems would come to light'.

Therefore, as Miss Bell acquired and studied her information, she was noticing discrepancies in the explanations which had been offered for the bruising and she picked up various warning signs. Not only was she studying the family interactions and feelings, she was also studying her own role in the situation.

Getting a more complete picture

The social worker studied a mass of facts, stories and impressions which she had picked up from a variety of people and sources.

The referral issue

Query non-accidental injury to a four-week-old baby: this was important in terms of there being a child at risk to which the agency had to respond.

The previous history

Miss Bell found out that there was a considerable history. There was available in the agency a small file on the mother which had relevance but there was no information about the father. There was a lot of material about the mother's family which was very relevant. There had been serious cases of non-accidental injury there too.

The family

There were several reasons why this factor was relevant:

(a) One assumes that mother has learned parenting from her parents; the kinds of parenting: control, expectations, attitudes to child-rearing, are likely to have been passed on to some extent—whether the reverse or the same. The same is true of the father. They are important in terms of the support system they provide for the family—are they a support or an additional stress factor.

(b) The other relevant factor was the bad feeling between the two halves of the family.

(c) Then the prime suspect (scapegoat?) for the whole thing turned out to be one of the father's brothers who lived in the same house who was said to be uncontrollable. He had terrible rages and was very unhappy at the child living there. This youth was fifteen and constantly truanted from school.

Agency function

The agency had a statutory duty to deal with this case, but the agency structure was also relevant:

I handled this case as the senior in the intake team because I was the most experienced in child abuse cases. It was handled by our team because we have an intake system in this area, so we would deal with emergency referrals automatically. We also have definite procedures for child abuse, and they work very well. Child abuse cases are very painful, very stressful, and bring out a lot of feelings in you, so you have to be very careful that you know what they are. It can be quite a painful learning experience for one. These fairly clear-cut procedures give some limits to hang on to emotionally. At that level I was not there to make decisions; though I did make decisions about the place of safety issue to give more time.

All child abuse cases have priority over anything else, and there must be a case conference within a few days of the incident to which everybody involved comes. By that time you must have done an assessment. You have 'to get your finger out' and see everybody as fast as possible. This means that you are absolutely inundated with gut feelings and information which you have to hold on to. Sometimes out of that mêlée of impressions, you find something quite valuable.

Personality factors

The baby had nothing unusual about him—he was not 'stroppy' or awkward. The parents were young, very keen to please authority and very dependent initially. Even so, Miss Bell found them 'very elusive':

> I would have been a lot happier with a big blow up at the beginning with all the feelings coming out, but they never did. They leaked out bit by bit and still are doing. Either they were as bewildered as I was, or they were hiding something and could not take the risk of getting too close.

The attitudes of the various parents were also studied against some norm:

> They were fairly standard for the district. The grandfather was very like father—still elusive, quite friendly, smiled a lot. Part of the time when he wanted to kick my face in, he was smiling. The grandmother was a lot straighter; when I first arrived she tore me off a strip. I felt she had quite a nasty temper and might nag a lot—a possible stress factor.

The social worker never saw the brother: 'He was raised as a spectre and remained one. I went several times when I hoped he would be in and he never was. I checked out about him at his school, where they told me he was a constant truanter and a problem'. The mother's parents were relevant too: 'I felt that in theory her mother was supposed to be supportive but in fact the baby's mother rarely went back home. I never discovered the reasons'. In fact, Miss Bell felt these were clues to quite a complex situation within this side of the family:

> I had got a picture of them as fairly caring people probably living in rather poor circumstances. Even so, I was quite surprised at what a low standard of housing it was. The house was filthy. The maternal grandmother looked very poorly, depressed and miserable, but there was a lack of fit between my expectations and the reality. The house was economically and socially poor. The picture I was presented was that all this does not matter—family solidarity matters more. But this, of course, can either work for or against you. From what she was saying, I got the impression of a good, solid, respectable although poor working-class family. But there were discrepancies. She talked

about this great family solidarity and then called her daughters like mad for letting their kids spoil her carpet. Double messages. She also told me about the baby's parents' courtship, how there was violence there and she had not wanted them to get married.

I got the impression that she was the boss in the household, although—and again this is culturally normal—she pushed her husband forward as the one who was the figurehead. She was quite a wild-looking woman and very dirty.

The most significant thing that came from the maternal grandmother's story was that nothing like this had ever happened in her family before and why should the social worker think any of them might have harmed the baby? Later, Miss Bell found out that this woman had covered up about her son's children who were now on the risk register. The other relevant story which came from the grandmother was the information about the previous violence between the baby's parents before they married.

Community and neighbourhood factors

There were a lot of children in care on the estate where this family lived.

They have a picture of what welfare is like—taking kids away from their parents—which is something you have to overcome when you get to an individual level with a family. That we are not there just to remove kids and keep them away and we are not only social policemen, although I think that is an inevitable part of the job in situations like this.

The sentencing policy of the court

The social services department had not involved the police at the beginning of this case:

The reason why was because I felt the parents were very vulnerable, that they knew that something had gone wrong and appreciated how serious it was, even though I found them elusive on another level. To bring the police in and 'double the tariff' would probably break up any chance of the child ever going home. I felt it would crack them completely. I also felt that if I could not find out who did it, then I did not think the police would be able to. The case went through the juvenile court rather than the adult court. The police were invited to the case conference. They had information about it having happened, but they would not go in unless they were called in.

Economic circumstances of the family

The father was on a very low wage and hated his job. His parents were both working; whilst they were not in dire economic stress, Miss Bell was surprised that their house was of such a low standard. Even so, it was relatively better than a lot of the houses on that estate. The young couple never had any money to go out anywhere, and the grandmother was not very keen on babysitting for them.

Health factors

Health factors were also relevant in this case. Though the mother had a heart condition, the birth had not presented problems and there was no sign of puerperal depression. Even so, the mother had had quite a rough pregnancy and had taken a risk in having the baby, given her heart defect. The pregnancy had been planned even though the mother was pregnant at the time of her marriage:

> What I found was against all my immediate reactions. They were really quite shocked at my impression that it had not been planned. They told me that they had been trying for a baby for a long time, but her mother would not let her get married. I wondered how much they were trying to force the issue, getting pregnant to get married against her mother's wishes. In fact it had not worked out that way. She got married as soon as she was eighteen and she was pregnant by then. She said she wanted a baby—that was how she saw her role in life—as a mother and child bearer and not a worker.

Miss Bell studied her data about the referral problem and the family's previous contact with social workers. She thought there was potential stress. Then there were problems and stresses in most areas of the family's life—economic and social circumstances, housing conditions, family relationships and interactions, personality and health issues. She also studied her own agency function and role very carefully before deciding how she would organise the continuing assessment. As she explained, there had to be several things going on at the same time:

> There was the immediate goal: I had to make sense of it, hold on to the procedure and get things to the court at the appropriate times. There was also the basic target for the parents. They had to feel that they were doing something that was likely to have an effect, otherwise they would have just lapsed into total apathy and depression.
> So there was a contract with them about visiting the child

and working with us. There were several alternatives for us to consider: let the place of safety order run out, supervision order, care orders, etc. Then there was the goal of making my assessment for the case conference and the court. My agency role came into this too. I work in an intake team and anything on which there is a case conference will probably become long-term anyway. I had to decide about what stage I would hand the case over to the long-term worker and the timing of introducing another worker. I have a lot of discretion, and I like to think the timing is a casework decision—when I feel the time is right.

Formulation

Miss Bell felt that the parents accepted her support and intervention and that they could use social work help in spite of being slightly elusive. She felt the case had to go to court for two reasons:

Firstly, although I felt that they would accept social work support, I am aware that I have made this mistake before of thinking that people would accept it and then finding out too late they were not as cooperative as I had expected. I wanted that sanction. Secondly, however 'nice' both sets of grandparents were being to my face, they were now gradually starting to sabotage it all. The grandmothers especially were doing a lot of undermining little things, playing on the mother's fears, and putting pressure on her to see child care in a coercive way. So, even if the parents were accepting me, the grandparents whom they respected were telling them not to trust social workers and to tell them as little as possible.

Miss Bell drew up a 'balance sheet' by considering the factors concerned with risk, need and resources. The *risk* to the baby was there but the social worker could not justify keeping him in care:

When I considered his long term prospects in care, I thought he had as good a chance at home. He could not stay with the foster mother for ever, and I would have no control over who a long-term foster mother would be. If his injuries had been terrible there would have been no question of his returning home. And I had no proof that either parents had ever injured this child. I also thought about natural justice and giving them the benefit of the doubt. And all the time this baby was getting older. In this case the risk did not override my assessment that he should return home.

115

The social worker could only think of risk in relation to resources:

> I recognised the risk with a four week old baby—if you shake a baby of that age, you can cause a brain haemorrhage. But we had a long term social worker who could devote time to the mother, plus offer resources (housing, Home-start, etc.). I was not really worried about what sort of quality of upbringing the mother was going to give him.

The social worker also realised that if the mother had hit the baby, it must have been because of housing/family stress, as her assessment was that the mother was basically very attached to her baby.

There were also *needs* in this case:

> The need I felt was for somebody to help the parents to strengthen the adult part of themselves. I had a choice: we could have put in an older female social worker who would have fulfilled the maternal role. The social worker who took the case was not so much older than the mother, but was a feminist, single, has a sense of humour and relates very well to girls of the mother's age. She could do a lot to strengthen the mother's own ability to manage things herself rather than encourage her to lean too much on others. It was more difficult for me to identify the father's needs. He related very well with me, used me as an authority figure and as an older sister—he had got a big enough mother of his own. Both parents had dominant mothers of their own about whom they were ambivalent and using a mother figure would have had its problems. To use a peer would be easier and probably more successful'.

Therefore, the evident risk and need were assessed in relation to the range and type of resources which were available.

Goal-setting

As we have seen, Miss Bell was clear that her major goal at this stage of her work was to produce an assessment for the case conference and the court, though she did have interim goals by having short-term aims for her work with the parents and organising certain interventions which were necessary for her assessment, such as the foster placement. The choices she was faced with were to:

1 Let the matter drop until the place of safety order ran out.
2 Take the case to court, if they had a case. The court could make:

(a) a supervision order—the child would return home under supervision but with definite limits.

or

(b) a care order—this could be dealt with in the following ways:
   (i) he could go home, with a lot of support and resources, with the parents knowing that the care order still existed; if they took one step out of line he would be taken away again and the local authority would have more rights in that situation.
   (ii) he could stay in local authority care until the parents had proved something, or until relationships had improved.

3 Receive the child into care (Section I) with the parents' sanction.

The social worker was aware of the differences between what people say they will do, and what they are able to do. The parents said that they would allow the child to be kept in care because they 'could see that they needed help'. 'But there is a difference between the way people feel with legal constraints and without'. There were arguments against most of the alternatives:

1 Allowing the place of safety order to lapse—Miss Bell was not sure how much future contact the grandparents would permit and she did not feel able to safeguard the child.
2 Against Section I—this had no legal sanction.
3 Supervision order—there was not enough control in the situation.
4 Child remaining in care:
   Against this was that the bonding could have been broken, and that if we had him in care now, I felt he was going to be in care for the rest of his life. I felt that to return him home at the age of two or three would increase, not lower, the chances of him being battered.

   In favour of him going home on a care order was the fact that I felt that basically they could offer reasonable care and that we would have the sanctions. What swung me was the risk factor, but that resource-wise I could do something about it: rehousing and social work intervention. I felt that we had as good an assessment as we could have had in the time (ten days) from myself and the health visitor.

There was a twenty-one day place of safety order in this case. Miss Bell wanted this period for time in order to complete her assessment and so that decisions could be made about social work help, rehousing and the availability of other resources for the family. The members of the case conference agreed with her assessment, and the recommendation for a care order, with the baby returning home to his parents in their own new house plus social work intervention. The court hearing was twenty-one days after the initial referral.

When the due date for the hearing arrived the case was not heard but was adjourned for twenty-eight days. Miss Bell's immediate aims were frustrated. She was angry at the adjournment because she had 'worked like mad' to complete her assessment on time, as well as to obtain housing through the co-operation of other departments. She had managed to obtain other resources for the family by the date of the court hearing. Miss Bell had to decide whether to let the baby go home before the end of the twenty-eight days, but realised that would reduce her chances of getting a care order:

> I would have had a very difficult job in court proving that I needed a care order to keep control of the situation if I had let the child go home before I got it. On the other hand, seven weeks was longer than the baby had spent with his natural parents, and in terms of his development, it was crucial that if he were going home he should go as soon as possible. I felt it was a terrible dilemma—whether I should let the baby go home and follow my social work instincts and jeopardise the chances of obtaining a care order which might put the baby at risk, or hold on to him and put the parents off. I dealt with it very unethically.

Miss Bell asked the housing department to hold the tenancy of the house until a week before the court appearance. The parents prepared the home by the time of the adjourned court hearing and they took the baby there that day. At the hearing a care order was made and the child went home, though there were still some complications.

> The parents initially told me that they were going to contest the care order—they were prepared to accept a supervision order. This was because the grandparents had been saying that he would be taken away any time. In view of that the child was separately represented. I jumped the gun of the 1975 Act. At present the child's solicitor is the parents' solicitor. In future, if the parents' rights and the child's rights are felt to conflict, the local authority can retain a solicitor on behalf of the child alone. The child's solicitor agreed with us. The parents' solicitor had a right to a hearing, but they had no right for any say in court.

Contracting was relevant in this case too:

> I made the contract about them visiting regularly, seeing me
> regularly and allowing me access to other members of their
> family. My part of it was basically that I would do as good an
> assessment as I could which would be as fair to them as
> possible. They kept pushing me to make a decision, but I told
> them that it was in no one's interest for me to make decisions
> in a hurry.

Miss Bell shared as much as she could with the parents as she
went along; the only specific thing she did not reveal to them was
delay in the housing provision. She explained her role and involvement very carefully and told them of their legal rights. She explained
what a place of safety order was and why this was being applied for.
She involved the parents in the baby's care at the foster-home. Even
so, she had to repeat what she was sharing with the clients and
sometimes wondered if she had clarified it enough.

Ultimately, the social worker did not have to ask the court's
permission for the child to go home—that was her decision; the care
order was the only issue that the court had the responsibility to
decide. In conclusion, Miss Bell commented:

> I stayed with, and had to stay with, the fact of a child with
> bruises. Everybody was saying to me, 'This has happened, it
> could never have happened, none of my children would do this,
> I would never do this.' I had to keep coming back to the four-
> week-old baby with bruises and no explanation, and it was not
> an accident. That was quite painful and quite hard work
> because there is a temptation to collude, especially when you
> have got over the first interview. People say to you, 'We have
> got over the hard stuff, let us get on with the relationship bit,
> help and support'. An unspoken contract, 'you get off our
> backs and we will co-operate'. I was helped by the fact of my
> assessment role. Because I was clear, I could be clear with the
> family. There is nothing upsets families in this situation more
> than social workers going all round the houses about what they
> are going to do. They prefer you to be straight about what you
> suspect and to face them with your dilemma. I think it is wrong
> to assume they cannot cope with it. But you have to have
> confidence in you ability to relate, and to have learned through
> discovering that you go through some awful experiences with
> clients and they reject you and you have done some awful
> things to them and you can still continue the relationship. No
> one can expect social workers who have just started to have
> that.

Case B An inquiry into a child's behavioural problems

Background

John Prince, aged eight, was referred by a local authority social worker to a university child treatment research unit for help with his 'disruptive' and 'bizarre' behaviour at home. He had previously been seen by a consultant psychiatrist within the school psychological service, but his parents felt that they needed more specific help with John's behaviour.

The unit is used by statutory and voluntary agencies as another service resource, but it has no statutory funding or responsibilities. It works mainly with motivated parents and their children. The director explained their approach:

> We tell people what the clinic does but clients do not put us into a clear-cut occupational pigeon hole. I think this is quite important, and has been explicitly so where some people have been resistant to social work intervention. This is particularly so with parents who live on so-called 'problem estates' where they often see the social worker as having a coercive statutory role.

Apart from the clinic's university and hospital connections, it derives its basic legitimation from its professionalism in parent-child problems. Its practitioners (specialising in behavioural casework) are seen as experts. The workers emphasise their research focus which has implications for the ways in which they attempt to understand and analyse their cases.

The referral

John's 'bizarre' behaviour was described in the following terms:

> John has a number of behaviours which do not fit into the normal pattern of an eight-year-old. The specific behaviours include such things as very very babyish talk and head rolling. However, his whole behaviour forms a role, he becomes a kind of comic so that he gets a lot of attention. But there comes a point where the silliness has got to stop and it is at that point that the parents feel he is uncontrollable. In addition his mother feels that he is now beginning to be labelled backward because of his silly talk and head rolling, but it is absolutely belied by John's behaviour in other situations.

John's 'disruptive' behaviour was described as aggression: 'He would throw things, or try to throttle his younger brother or do quick kicks. This was less of a problem at home than it was at school'.

The local authority worker also provided information about the family's previous contact with social workers. The parents had seen a consultant children's psychiatrist and a psychiatric social worker some years previously. They had been dissatisfied with this contact because the focus was on their marital problems rather than on John's behaviour.

The referral was accepted for assessment. The assessment work undertaken was shared by the director and a student social worker. They made three visits of observation to the home, seven visits were made for assessment purposes. Psychometric tests were also carried out. The social workers started their assessment with an open mind about both the existence and the nature of the problem, but they hypothesised about possibilities:

> I would go into a new situation with a notion that there are distressing interactions going on, but that the child's behaviour might very well be quite appropriate. I do not go in with the notion that I am definitely going in to treat, or that there is definitely going to be a problem within the child.

Acquisition and study of information

The local authority social worker had provided information about the previous history and the presenting problem. Most of this was checked during the subsequent visits to the home and systematic data were gathered about John's developmental history and his current situation. The series of visits and observational exercises were part of the process of assessment and not undertaken merely to obtain factual information. Data were gathered about numerous areas of John's life and attempts were made to study them in relation to the problem-definition and the family's feelings about the situation.

The behaviour which was defined as a problem

The workers visited the home to see John's behaviour and interaction within his family. They wanted also to see how far the behaviours they observed and were investigating fitted the mother's reporting of them. The workers used a formula to examine the frequency, intensity, number, duration and sense (FINDS) of the behaviour. They found out what led to the behaviour (the antecedents), what the specific piece of behaviour comprised (behaviour) and what were the responses to it (consequences) (ABC):

> We were looking at the frequency and we also got mum to record the times and rate with which his 'problem' behaviours occurred. We were trying to specify the behaviour. We asked mum to suggest two major categories and she came up with

121

aggressive and silly behaviours. We then split these down into actual observable actions, such as throwing, kicking, exaggeratedly nodding his head and doing a silly walk. Through observation, talking, description and recording we got a picture of what John's current behaviour was like; also its situation-specificity and the contingent reinforcers maintaining it. This also included a talk at school with his headmaster and teacher.

John's mother was an invaluable source of information to the workers:

A lot of behaviour may occur at a time when we cannot observe it because we change the behaviour simply by being there. Some-times it does not change when you get to know the child well and you see him. We are trying to get the mother to use her own eyes in the way that we would be using our eyes if we could be there. We teach her to record his specific behaviours, using the FINDS and ABC headings, and this includes the sense both the child and the parents make of what is happening.

As the workers gathered their data on John's problem behaviour, they were beginning to see more clearly the sequences in his behaviour:

Behaviour is learned and has a sequence: antecedents and consequences. We began to train the mother to think in these terms by keeping a diary of each event, so that she could see if there was a pattern developing. In this way parents begin to see the inter-relation of their behaviour and those of their children. We also included the father in this.

The workers thought the mother was particularly observant: 'She remarked quite early on that in observing and recording she was beginning to see patterns and was beginning to anticipate in some instances'. The workers then had to begin to decide whether John's behaviour was really problem behaviour per se or just behaviour which his parents regarded as problematic:

In the end we have to make a social judgment obviously. Is John's behaviour such that it would necessitate some inter-vention, or is it the sort of behaviour which, within his chrono-logical and mental age, and developmental norms, and considering his own progress, is quite satisfactory.

In these terms we found that at the level that John was using bizarre behaviour, it really necessitated some intervention from us. We took into account the social implications of what he was doing and one of the most important factors was that he was becoming labelled in school as maladjusted. Such an out-come would have been very unfortunate for everyone.

The major issues were the implications of the exaggeration and inappropriateness of John's behaviours in terms of his social setting. His father was important in this respect, but his school was also a factor.

He goes to a school for delicate children. In a normal school playground his aggressive behaviour—a quick thump and a kick—is not really a problem. But in a school for delicate children it is more of an issue because it can have serious consequences for children with delicate bones, asthma and hemiplegia.

The problem definition in this situation was quite complex and included the tolerance thresholds of other people:

There is always a balance and we would probably decide on the evidence whether we need to change the child's behaviour or the attitudes and tolerance thresholds of the people around him. With delicate children there is very little 'give' in the system and the best we can do is to try and make the child alter his own behaviour.

In some respects, the headmaster was quite right—that within that school John's behaviour was a problem.

The frequency and intensity of John's behaviours were also a problem because of his school setting. But the sense or meaning (for him) of his behaviour also had to be taken into account:

His role as the buffoon may in some ways have helped him to overcome his rather awkward posture and rather large head; to remove any comic elements itself would simply not be John any more. His mum said that she would be very upset if that were to happen.

Therefore, John's behaviour was not studied in isolation from the role he played and the feelings he and his parents had about this.

The workers did not only consider problem behaviour, they also took account of John's pro-social behaviour. John seemed also to have positive aspects: His comic role was pro-social because he sometimes creates a good atmosphere. He is also intelligent and generous and can engage in both serious and amusing conversation without any of his problematic behaviour happening. The workers commented that they were fortunate in their work with John's family, because they were able to see and give weight to the positives and this is not the case in all families where there is a 'difficult' child. The positives in the family situation were stressed by the social worker who referred the case.

John's behaviour was studied in a very systematic way. After examining its nature and meaning and the family's feelings about the 'problem', it seemed as if John's disruptive and aggressive behaviour was something which could be worked on without changing either his personality or his pro-social habits.

John's previous history

The developmental history turned out to be extremely important in this case. A child's developmental history from birth, including his physical milestones and attachment behaviours, often provides some sort of eye-opener into possible historical antecedents of negative and coercive interactions between him and his family:

> In this case the birth itself was problematic, because it was a three-day labour. He suffered from lack of oxygen at birth which was the cause of the hemiplegia. The mother immediately thought there was something wrong with John and refused to see him at first until the father persuaded her to do so. He had many difficulties: gross feeding problems, poor sleep patterns and limbs which did not work properly. So right from the beginning he might be said to have high 'demand characteristics' and was getting a lot of intensive interaction with his mother. We were beginning to understand the reinforcement history of the parent child attachment system because it helps to explain present patterns, how they become established and why they are so difficult to shift if we, by negotiation, agree that they need shifting. Part of our function as a university research unit (as well as a service clinic) is to try and understand what is happening.

This kind of historical investigation and the knowledge which comes from it can also be liberating for parents:

> We think it serves as a really useful part of interaction with the parents because it begins to show to them that from the beginning they were having difficulties with the child because he was demanding attention purely in a life and death manner. In order to get him fed and to sleep, his mother had to be with him all the time.

Despite this, the picture of John's history was not all darkness and gloom: 'His mother was intelligent and perceptive. Although she had given him a lot of attention, she tried to hold back—to let him develop himself and use his limbs'.

There had been marital difficulties between John's parents but the mother felt that these were not abnormally different from other people's marriage problems and John had shown no serious acting-out behaviours as a result of them. The assessment at this point might have widened out to investigate more intimate aspects of the family interaction, but the workers decided not to explore the marital problems, but rather to put it 'in the back of our minds as of possible relevance later'. However, within the fairly recent history, the marital problems did have some generalised effect on John, because he was old enough and intelligent and sensitive enough to participate in some of the things which were going on. The workers consciously and on theoretical grounds decided not to keep the marital problems in the forefront of their work, because these did not seem to be connected with John's *specific* behavioural difficulties, though the problems could have relevance in the subsequent treatment if they prevented a concerted programme of work by the parents.

Another significant factor in John's history was that his father had been in prison, and during this period the behavioural sequences increased in level and intensity. This had serious repercussions for the whole family:

> While father was in prison some quite interesting things happened. This was the time that the social services became involved because Mrs Prince was very depressed, felt John was very difficult to cope with and asked for him to be taken into care. Social services workers felt that she was using this as a manipulative technique to get more visits to the prison, because they interpreted John's behaviour as trying to get to prison to see his dad.

John's behaviour was understandable, as the workers explained:

> John really wanted to see his father and worked out that if he burned the house down, his dad would have to come home to build the house again (he was a builder). Either that or he thought he would be sent to prison where he could be with his dad.

Mrs Prince became very depressed; she was unsuccessful in obtaining extra prison visits so that John could see his father more often. John's behaviour deteriorated; it was a very bad time for the mother and she felt that the only way out was to have John taken into care. The social worker placed John on the risk register as a precaution and maintained contact with the family. She also arranged a voluntary baby sitter for Mrs Prince, and this proved extremely helpful. Altogether, the probation officer and social worker were regarded positively by all concerned, and it was felt that their supportive work had helped to hold the family together, but that something more was now required. The father's criminality *per se* was not examined during this assessment, it was only felt to be an issue in terms of the effects on John's previous behaviour.

Therefore, there were many problem areas in John's history. He had had a difficult time from birth and this seemed to have some bearing on his interactional and behavioural deficits; even so, there were many positives in his favour. There had been marital problems between his parents, but these were given a low profile except in terms of their more general consequences for John's behaviour. They were not considered to be important in terms of specific determinants of the target behaviours. John's father had been in prison and this was seen as relevant only in terms of the specific behavioural consequences for the boy and his mother at that time.

Family

John's behaviour was examined in the context of his family, not only in order to make sense of it in social-learning theory terms but also in order to identify why his behaviour was seen as a problem by his relatives:

> We looked at attachment systems. We found that he is very close to his mum and some of his behaviours are very low in frequency when she is around; the same also happened when father was around, so when he was away in prison, there was a heightening of all his behaviours. However, when they were outside the home, then neither mother nor father seemed to have control over him. The mother seemed to be the stronger one of the two. She is more articulate and dominant in conversation. Father had to be encouraged to draw out his ideas. His six-year-old brother seemed fine, bright and lively. But a lot of the problem is with John's interaction with his brother. We observed what they were like together; and found John being extremely good and the brother acting up. However, their mother told us this was not the brothers' normal behaviour and was for our benefit.

So the family was assessed in a specific rather than a general manner:

> We concentrated on the assessment of the behaviour; literally second-by-second accounts of certain kinds of behaviour and a close analysis of it in learning/developmental terms. We were trying to tease out the specificity of it—with whom, at what times—a pedantic worrying away at it.

Though there were problems in John's family, their particular implications for his 'difficult' behaviour had to be examined in specific detail.

Personality

John was a warm, generous child with a vivid imagination and he was academically bright. He was very sensitive to attitudes at home, but also quite independent. Even so, the unit workers paid very little attention to such a broad category as 'personality':

> In terms of our theoretical questioning of the child's problems we spend little time on his personality traits—especially with conduct problems. Don't children have personalities? Of course they have personalities in the popular sense but we find that the generality of attitudes has very little predictive value in what we do—especially when it comes to younger children. We are more concerned with the specificity of behaviour in particular contexts and the controlling contingencies associated with them.

John's personality was not discounted in this assessment, but it took a low profile compared with the specificity of his behaviours which created problems for himself and others.

Community and neighbourhood

These factors were taken into account in terms of how the class and community background of the family affected their expectations of the child; these were the contexts in which John would have to survive. John was a member of two communities. He belonged to the community of the physically disabled and that had important implications for the decisions that would be taken in respect of intervention. John was also a member of a neighbourhood which was both a problem and a help to him. He had to be careful of the traffic and sometimes his friends down the road were put off by his kicking and grabbing. On the other hand he was a member of the cubs where he was accepted and which he thoroughly enjoyed. But John was a member of a working-class family and it was important to realise that some children have to be aggressive in order to survive in some difficult situations, though this did not seem to be relevant with John. John's family had open contacts with the community, in terms of relatives, neighbours and clubs. They were not isolated.

Class factors were also relevant in terms of socialisation:

> According to the literature, middle-class mums tend to be much more inductive in their child-rearing methods—lots of

127

explanations and discussion. The strange thing is that when we suggest things to parents with excessively attention-seeking children, we suggest what are allegedly working-class methods of control—fewer explanations, discussions and endless disputes.

Therefore class factors in child-rearing techniques had to be examined and either changed or, in John's case, reinforced.

Economic circumstances of the family

The family was in receipt of social security but they were considered to be financially reasonably secure. Whilst they did not have a comfortable stable income, there was no evidence of gross need. Their economic circumstances did not seem to be relevant to the behavioural problems.

School

John went from the beginning to a school for the physically handicapped because of his asthma and hemiplegia. There were no problems academically and in that respect it would have been appropriate for him to go out to an ordinary school. This did not happen because his teachers thought he was, 'not quite, absolutely normal', and his mother was concerned that he would become the butt of vicious attacks because of 'silly behaviours' if he went to another school.

The workers planned a school visit in order to negotiate what kind of behaviour could be accommodated in John's school, but they had to be careful because they were crossing the boundaries of the school psychological service functions. This was very important because, if their intervention failed, John was likely to be placed in a school for maladjusted children and few people thought this would be appropriate. School factors had particular significance in John's case because his behaviour punished him in two ways—it stopped him going to an ordinary school and it was influencing decisions for him to go to a school for maladjusted children.

Health

As we have seen, John had quite a lot of health problems—a wandering eye, one deaf ear, hemiplegia, asthma and eczema. Most of these problems were medically well controlled. However, the integrity of John's nervous system had been adversely affected by anoxia:

The metaphor we keep using about him is a 'motor car without brakes'. When he starts up, he gains momentum and has no self control—he does not know where to end the situation. Therefore we want to do a little bit of explaining to the mother about the intrinsic sources of his problems, but also to put more emphasis on teaching the child self-control.

John's many medical difficulties were well controlled except for his continuing volatility.

Disability has wider implications than health and medical problems:

You find with a lot of physically or mentally disabled children that they are slow to learn the nuances of socially appropriate behaviour. This is an area where we would like to do some developmental counselling with John's mother, because he is not emotionally disturbed in any qualitative sense—he is an ordinary child (albeit physically disabled) who has got problems. He is capable of learning pro-social or antisocial behaviour according to the same principles as other non-disabled youngsters.

There were many issues, signs and consequences of John's behavioural difficulties which, by careful assessment, could be analysed in fine detail. John, thought of holistically, was not all 'problem', but there were aspects of his specific behaviour which had profound implications for him, his family, his school and his friends. Some of his problems were medically controlled whilst others required the learning of more self-control on his part and management advice for his parents. If he were to be helped, his parents had to become partners in the treatment:

In the child treatment research unit, one of the things I like is that I am not necessarily doing what one calls therapy, because it is the parents who are in there to mediate change. This is how we get into the child's life-stream so-to-speak; we teach the parents, so that they will initiate and maintain long-term socialisation developments, but only those to which they agree. They are treating me as an expert, but I am passing on something they can use. The techniques and ideas behind it are so basic to the way people behave, that if you can leave them with the tools to do it, they will not need the experts afterwards.

In this case, the workers were locating factors in the interaction between the environment and John; he had been reinforced for certain behaviours, but his own particular make-up (the organismic factors) had also drawn out certain behaviours from the environment. There were two dimensions which were relevant. One was the historical past and its causal relevance for current behaviour. The other was the here and now, current events which were maintaining and instigating behavioural problems.

The workers' study of facts and feelings in John's situation led them to identify the problem behaviour, its source, meaning and consequences, in great detail. As they were studying and assessing, they were anticipating the possibilities of future intervention. They actively involved the parents in their assessment and plans:

> At this stage you are half-way through the negotiations, because we say to parents, 'If I had a magic wand and could change the child, what would be the most important to you?' In this way we are getting a hierarchy of the problems as the parents see them in their desire for change. We act as advocates for the child—spokesmen for his point of view—even though it may not agree with parents' priorities.

Formulation

As we have indicated throughout this book, the study stage of any assessment process is not an *ad hoc* collection of facts, even though we have to present it in this arbitrary way at a certain stage in our exposition. In the assessment of John a balance sheet was drawn up in which an attempt was made to weigh the various factors which had been studied.

First, the workers gave priority to John's behaviour in its context. They tried to work out the implications if John maintained his behaviour and decided that he was a high *risk* case if change was not attempted. His behaviour was labelling him and channelling him into the maladjusted role through the school system. In terms of his own personal development, he was going to be perceived by most people in the outside world as mentally retarded and that did him an injustice. John was not a high risk in terms of what was happening to the family because he was well accommodated in a loving family. He was at risk in terms of his personal and social development if nothing was done to help him overcome his behavioural difficulties.

Second, there was evidence of *need*. John's mother felt that she wanted some help to control her son, not only to make life more pleasant for herself and the family, but also for John's own development. At one stage the mother asked for John to be received into care, and this again was an indication of her need for assistance. Children rarely conceptualise themselves as in need of help and the workers assumed a kind of advocacy for this child: 'Children are so unreflexive when they are very young, that we have to find out whether the parents are making unreasonable demands on the child. We did not think this was the case with John'.

The workers had to be very specific about their definitions of need. John's mother was very clear that she did not want his personality to be changed. She told the workers that she did not want them to make John into something different or to take away his nice, warm, comic element. So John's specific needs were identified, the parents wanted help with them and the behaviour was potentially modifiable.

Third, risks and needs must always be considered in terms of available *resources*. Resources were assessed quite consciously in two ways:

> Although there might be high need and high risk in the family, it may be that the interactions or abilities within the family are such that they could not necessarily use a very strict, systematic programme. We may be able to change our approach in that situation, but we always look at how the parents are going to be able to cope with a fairly rigorous programme as well. Therefore, our baseline period is not just an assessment of a baseline against which to make a change, but also a testing of resourcefulness of the parents to stick to certain rules.

It was felt that the parents were sufficiently resourceful to work with a behavioural programme. The resources in the clinic also had to be considered. In this case a student social worker was able to begin work with John's family.

The risks of non-intervention were high, there were needs in the family for which the mother was seeking help, and there were appropriate resources for help to be offered in relation to both the risk and the need. However, the workers found it difficult to come to this conclusion:

> The main problem was to get down to what the behaviours were and the ethical aspects of balancing them for John. We had to ensure that if we were to intervene, we were not going to do something that was seriously wrong, taking away things that may be and are very essential to him.

The formulation had also taken into account alternative options. First, the workers rejected non-intervention because they felt they had the resources to help and there was not much chance of spontaneous remission. Second, receiving John into care was never considered. Third, child guidance was rejected because John's family had had a very unhappy experience of that, and the workers had assessed that the marital problem did not seem to be shaping John's behaviour. Fourth, if social services surveillance had continued, John would probably be moved to a school for maladjusted children. Fifth, family aids were considered but John's mother was not asking for that kind of help. Sixth, clinical psychology might have helped, but John would not have been accepted at the paediatric assessment centre because care had been taken of his physical problems. John could have obtained psychological help but that would have been similar to the help the unit was offering. The most likely alternative would have been continued contact from the social services department, but John's mother was rejecting that and asking for something extra. The unit workers thought they were the right people to help as they had exactly what was needed, in the light of the alternatives which were considered.

Goal-setting

Preparing a report for another agency or service is not a major objective in the child treatment research unit, though in some cases the workers write reports for other professionals. The goal set at the conclusion of the assessment of John was that they could intervene to try to alter some of the interactions between John and his parents. They could work with John at a cognitive level to try to establish in him a greater measure of self-control, and they could alter some of the controls from his environment, including his parents' reactions to the changes. The goals at the assessment stage were set in the broad terms of self-control and environmental control. Such broad goals would then have to be operationalised during the intervention stage of their work. For example, one of the problems was to change some of the reinforcements in John's environment because some of his silly behaviours received a lot of attention. John would be helped to see particular situations as either not producing certain kinds of reinforcement or not being as threatening as he believed. The workers would suggest to the mother what to do when certain behaviours were seen to occur. The goals which were set at the end of the assessment stage were only broadly defined but would have to be operationalised in more specific terms and those goals would be renegotiable during the intervention stages of the work.

The workers shared much of their assessment with John's parents, though it was rather more difficult to share it with John. They had to make it clear to John that they were not there to 'take him away'. However, there are many ways of communicating with children. These include projective techniques, discussion, games, role-play and tapes. The workers did not make a written contract with John and his parents, but they made a verbal agreement. They involved the parents and John in decisions about actual behaviours, rewards and punishments. For example, John wanted a baked potato as one reward for his efforts.

The assessment stage in this case was analytically quite distinct from the intervention and evaluation phases. Even so, the workers acknowledged that they were also intervening as they were assessing. Whilst they were establishing their baseline with John and his parents, some of the problem behaviours were beginning to change:

> As the mother began to discuss and record John's behaviour, she began to see them in a different light. She began to anticipate what was bringing on the behaviour and to see the consequences. So the actual programme begins before the official intervention, even though we try to give as little advice as possible during the assessment period.

Therefore, assessment is the beginning of the change and the relationship is established between the workers and the clients through their shared work.

The workers had to draw a fine balance in this case between too much or too little intervention:

> We had to be extremely careful. I feel reasonably confident that we have at least got to the core of what is going on, but realise that we have to be careful not to intervene too much. I was worried that we might be so efficient and reduce the behaviour so much that, if we were not careful, it would backfire and would not benefit anyone at all. So it has to be modulated.

The workers thought that intervention could be effective, because there were many hopeful signs: they had a reasonably accurate story, there was a high motivation for change and there were adequate resources. Even so, the workers were aware of the ethical implications of what they were doing:

> A physically handicapped child has many things in his socialising experiences that make life difficult. We must be so careful, because if a child is surviving, as this child is, as a physically handicapped child, the awful reality he has to learn to cope with has helped survival. They are functional in one way and dysfunctional in another sense. Awfully critical de-cisions fall on our shoulders and on his parents' shoulders if we are saying that behaviours which are functional in the short run are dysfunctional in the long run for the child. We have a level of detailed analysis which makes for a more rigorous discussion of the ethical issues than would have been possible if we had left it all rather vague and general.

Case C   An inquiry into the discharge from hospital of a terminally ill patient

This example relates to a hospital social worker's assessment and intervention with a terminally-ill patient. The central client was a middle-aged woman who had been in the hospital for some time before the work described below was undertaken.

Because of the nature of the inquiry the overall assessment process contained several interim assessments and therefore the four stages are not as neatly divided in this case. Each of the interim assessments sees the worker obtaining information, considering it, weighing up the client's position and setting goals as she works with the client.

Background

Mrs Brown is a social worker in a large general hospital and has special responsibility for the medical wards, where many of the patients are terminally ill. She has close contacts with the medical and nursing staff; she goes through all the cases with the sister to check if there is any patient whose circumstances may need investigation. Because Mrs Brown is so well-known to the staff, she is in regular contact with the terminal care units and people trust her: 'They see what I can do and therefore they let me do more. You are allowed to do as much as people see you are able to do'.

The case of Mrs Simpson was a fairly ordinary referral. She was a woman in her fifties who had inoperable cancer and was going to die in the next few months. The ward staff wanted to know about her home situation before she was discharged and to ascertain if any practical help was required. The staff did not envisage any problem because they saw Mr and Mrs Simpson as middle-class people who would cope; they had a secure income, had many friends and it was thought that it would be a straightforward matter to arrange for her to go home. This was the level at which Mrs Brown accepted the referral:

> I thought that sounded fine. I knew the area and the road in which she was living, so I knew the sort of house from which she came. I knew a little bit about the family and the social support she was receiving from her friends.

Given the information about the case which Mrs Brown had obtained from the medical notes and from the ward sister, she went to her first interview with Mrs Simpson with an open mind:

> When going to an assessment of that kind, I am always thinking on two levels. Firstly, the home situation looked as if it might be straightforward. Secondly, this was someone who I

knew was likely to die in the near future and therefore there may be family complications later on. I was not at all sure what either the family or Mrs Simpson knew. Therefore, I was thinking about both the practical and the emotional implications of the illness.

Mrs Brown then arranged her first interview with Mrs Simpson, who told her that she wanted to go home:

> She was very sure that everything could be provided and everything was all right. She was very prickly and felt it a bit of an insult that she had a social worker seeing her. This was not something that people living in that area had, so I explained to her that I see all ready-for-home patients as a courtesy measure.

Mrs Brown became aware of other factors during the first interview. First, though Mrs Simpson looked reasonably well physically, she could not get her breath. Second, it seemed that she did not really know how ill she was because she was so busy telling the social worker how well she was:

> I did not necessarily think she was being defensive, because in a sense she had been told the truth about the operation being successful. What she had not been told was the the lung cancer had spread and was inoperable. Her GP had just said that she had now got a chest infection which needed treatment in hospital. So her reactions were fairly logical rather than defensive.

The factual information and some less tangible indications to which the social worker was alerted at this stage were beginning to suggest a rather more complex story. First, there was little which could be provided physically that the family did not already have. Second, Mrs Simpson probably could not cope at home; her plans were unrealistic given the medical prognosis, but she did not know how ill she was. It was necessary to find out how much the husband knew about his wife's medical condition. Third, the social worker wanted to find out more about the family's coping abilities at an emotional and social level:

> Mrs Simpson had indicated a little bit during this first interview that things might not be so easy. She was worried about how she would manage because her husband was so hopeless at cooking and other household tasks. She had a daughter living nearby but she was expecting a baby.

So, as the social worker was studying facts and feelings in this case, she was beginning to build up a picture of a family with resources but who might have some problems in coping with the particular circumstances facing them.

Therefore, at this first study stage, the social worker decided that she wanted to find out from the husband how much he knew about Mrs Simpson's medical prognosis and what were his coping abilities. Further care could be planned in the light of this assessment. So Mrs Brown told Mrs Simpson that it would help if she could just discuss with her husband what could be provided:

> I almost never see relatives without the patient's permission. I think in hospital it is too easy to go behind people's backs without either giving them a chance to refuse or, if they cannot do that, at least to ask them why. I wanted to establish some credibility with Mrs Simpson and to have some reason to see her again without upsetting her.

Mrs Brown had made an *interim assessment* at this stage. She had by now cancelled out the practical matters as an issue, and had decided that what she really wanted to know was whether Mrs Simpson and her husband wanted her to die at home. She had to see Mr Simpson to find that out. She told the ward staff of her plans, which they understood and the discharge was postponed. At this stage, therefore, Mrs Brown had to intervene in order to continue her assessment.

Mrs Brown then interviewed Mr Simpson on his own in the hospital. Immediately she discovered that he was not aware of the severity of his wife's illness and had at no time discussed it with a doctor:

> I knew very easily and very soon that Mr Simpson was unaware how ill his wife was. He was very much a professional man— stiff upper lip. He told me that he had been to a school where he was taught never to show his feelings. He was very competent, very willing to talk about his wife and what could be organised. But he was talking totally unrealistically about it. So I soon realised that this man was expecting his wife to at least show some improvement.

So, Mrs Brown saw that she had to arrange for Mr Simpson to see the doctor before the assessment could continue:

> I felt there was no point in my interviewing and discussing anything until he had been told the truth. Until one member of the family at least knew the situation, we were all working in a fantasy world that was not going to happen.

She asked Mr Simpson if he would like to see the doctor as it would help to discuss his wife's illness: this was agreed and arranged almost immediately. Mrs Brown asked Mr Simpson if he would like her to sit in on the interview and he agreed. Mrs Brown also prepared the doctor for the interview beforehand and more or less told him what to say—that Mr Simpson should be given the facts about his wife's illness and prognosis and some information about the possible nature of the deterioration.

Mr Simpson—not surprisingly—was very shocked at the doctor's news:

> He came in, expecting a reinforcement of the fact that his wife still had cancer and that was a very sad thing. He looked anxious but reasonably relaxed, comfortable and still very much in control of himself. When the registrar explained that the disease had spread, he then, after a pause, asked how long his wife had got. When the registrar said about two months, he became quite rigid. He was quite shattered, did not burst into tears, but there was a terrific tension. He could not believe it, just sat and said nothing for a few minutes.

Mr Simpson was particularly shocked as he understood from his family doctor that, though the cancer was inoperable, his wife might live about two years. Immediately, he backtracked and said, 'Oh yes, that is all right, I can organise things now I know where I stand. I shall take my wife home. Thank you very much'.

The doctor left Mr Simpson with the social worker. Mrs Brown thought he was emotionally vulnerable, not only because of his reality situation but also because he seemed unable to show his feelings.

At this stage in her assessment, Mrs Brown was beginning to understand the emotional interaction in the Simpson family, and she wanted to help them cope at a feeling level with their sad news:

> What I felt at this stage was that there was a woman on the ward who I knew was going to die and I had responsibility for providing some sort of care when she left hospital, if ever she did. There was a man who had just been given shattering information about his wife, who was in a sense wanting to withdraw both himself and his wife. I felt that I must hang on at all costs, because this was a very natural immediate reaction. I needed to explain just what there was because I was not sure that they could just cope.

Therefore, Mrs Brown began to share with Mr Simpson possible sources of help at home and also the terminal care unit and other nursing homes. She knew from experience that the only knowledge he would retain from the interview was likely to be the prognosis. She therefore invited him to contact her again:

There were two ways he could cope with those two months. I
did not want him to fix a period in his mind and either exist in
those two months or cut them out completely and deny them. I
wanted them to be able to live in that time and for him to
recognise that she was still living.

Mrs Brown thought that it would have been totally inappropriate
just then to persuade Mr Simpson to focus on practicalities because
his immediate response had been that he could cope and wanted
to take her home. She wanted him to go home, talk with his
family, think about it and grieve privately. Then, if he still wanted to
take her home, they would be able to plan in a more realistic and
objective way.

Mr Simpson telephoned Mrs Brown the following day, saying that
he could not cope with his wife at home and wanted her admission to
the terminal care unit. Mrs Brown remembered what the wife had
told her about Mr Simpson's lack of household skills, and thought
that he seemed unable at that time to gain emotional support
himself in order to care for his wife. She thought that he had not
allowed himself enough time to think it all through.

Mrs Brown suggested that Mr Simpson met her later that day at
the terminal care unit so that he could see it and assess it for his
wife's needs. She could also use that opportunity to discuss Mrs
Simpson's reaction to the possible transfer, and to follow up the
previous day's discussion with the doctor.

Mr Simpson also asked Mrs Brown if she would communicate the
prognosis to his wife because he could not tell her. Mrs Brown
arranged to see Mrs Simpson. The main factors gathered and
confirmed at this interview were that Mrs Simpson knew that she
had had cancer in the past, and that her mother and sister had died
of cancer in a terminal care unit: she was intelligent and articulate
and would want accurate information. Therefore, Mrs Brown began
to share with Mrs Simpson some of the facts and feelings about her
situation:

I started by saying that I had seen her husband, as she knew,
and we had discussed how they would manage if she went
home. She was deteriorating slightly, was more breathless and
had had a bad patch. This was helpful to me because I was
able to use that and say to her, 'Look, you are not really well
enough to cope at home are you?' She was able to acknowledge
something as concrete as that.

Mrs Brown began then to discuss Mrs Simpson's condition in
more detail. She did not attempt to deny the fact that medically
nothing more could be done, but did not indicate the possible length

of time because that would have been too overwhelming for Mrs Simpson at that point; the doctors also needed to be consulted before such information could be given. Mrs Brown also referred back to some of the things that Mrs Simpson had told her at the first interview. For example:

> I mentioned that she had said her husband found it a bit difficult cooking, that she worried about him, and that her children were tied up with their own family matters. Perhaps, therefore, it seemed more appropriate for the moment to think of a transfer to the Memorial Hospital. When she knew where it was, she said 'That is it, is it not? This is the end; I am going to die; they only send people there if they are going to die'. I did not deny this. It is not use saying, 'No, no, you are not going to die'; equally, I did not say, 'Yes, you are'. I think it is important just to be there and be quiet for a while.

Mrs Simpson just lay back on her pillows and Mrs Brown sat quietly with her. However, at the same time, the social worker was privately setting goals and planning ahead. She then said to Mrs Simpson,

> Yes, people do die at the Memorial Hospital. I know your relatives died there. But they can also do other things like pain control'. Mrs Simpson became interested in that. I was also able to make her a promise that, even if it was only for a short period of time, she could go home for a day or a weekend. I did not want her, like her husband, to just give up, thinking, 'I am dead now'.

Some terminal patients need to share their feelings about dying, and Mrs Brown discussed this with Mrs Simpson at this stage in the assessment process:

> Mrs Simpson told me that she knew she was dying, she was not afraid of death itself but felt that she was a coward. She had seen her mother and her sister die from cancer and she was terrified that she would show herself up. That was all very positive for me because I was able to reassure her that she would certainly be able to die with dignity and with no pain.

Mrs Brown used her previous knowledge as she shared Mrs Simpson's fears about death:

> Many patients want to talk about the process of dying. Will they be breathless? Will they be in terrible pain? These questions rather than the fact of not being alive. I know from the type of illness they have, how they are likely to be. It is

important to be honest about it, because it is no good pretending it is going to be nice and peaceful if it is not going to
be.

The hospital setting also helped the social worker at this painful
communication stage of the assessment:

One of the joys and the easier aspects of hospital interviews is
that you can see people daily so that they are not left for a long
period wondering what they have told you. They also see you on
the ward talking to other people and so it is acceptable.

Various plans had been drawn up at this stage. Mrs Simpson saw
her transfer to the Memorial Hospital as a means of obtaining pain
control. She knew that her husband was going to visit the hospital
with a view to reporting on it both to her and to Mrs Brown. In the
meantime, Mrs Simpson said that she would like Mrs Brown to
continue to see her daily to talk generally about her circumstances.

As Mrs Brown was formulating her assessment in this case, the
balance sheet seemed very clear:

The things that I had been able to write off were the things like
going home and practical help. We had cleared that part out of
the way. We had arranged her transfer to the unit and we also
had some plans in terms of getting her home somehow. The
resource factor was an issue, because she had to wait a further
two weeks before going to the terminal care unit. Therefore, I
needed to discuss with the ward staff the fact that I had made
the decision that this patient should not go home for several
reasons. This meant that a hospital bed was going to be
blocked.

Mrs Brown saw the husband at the terminal care unit and twice
again on his own at the hospital. She realised that Mr Simpson was
not going to move a long way in terms of feelings, but that he was able
to go along with the plans for the terminal care unit and his wife's
visits home. When she concluded her assessment, the social worker
was clear about her goal-setting plans which were: to help Mr and
Mrs Simpson to communicate with each other about the situation;
to enable Mrs Simpson to return home if possible, after the pain
control had been established; to offer emotional support to them
individually in order to talk through the trauma.

At this stage of the work, the assessment and intervention
processes were merging. Whilst Mrs Simpson was waiting to be
transferred, Mr Brown wanted to use the waiting time to clear many
things out of the way:

The time had to be used so that Mrs Simpson did not feel

nothing was being done. She was anxious to go, wanted to go and was asking about her transfer every day. I also had to help the houseman to know how to approach her because he was very wary of doing this when she knew she was dying. So I had a special session with him on how to talk to patients.

Mrs Brown indicated her plans to Mr and Mrs Simpson:

I gave Mrs Simpson the opportunity of talking about her husband, talking very realistically about the fact that he could not show his feelings and how he wished he could. I helped her to realise that it was possible to show feelings and to discuss such things as dying on the public ward.

Mrs Brown also set in motion the agreed plans for Mrs Simpson to go home.

He agreed to take her home on Sunday for the afternoon so that they could be alone together there. She found it helpful to discuss this with me, and they were able to share something on their own. She also wanted to discuss such things as what she would do with her jewellery, but she wanted to test it out with me first.

In that situation it was also important to remain aware of the reality of the terminal illness, and this had implications for the nature of the interviews done. Mrs Brown aimed at making each interview complete in itself. She was careful to deal with the patient's feelings so that each interview ended on a positive, hopeful note because Mrs Simpson might not live for another meeting. At the same time the worker needed to have an ongoing plan of work because Mrs Simpson's life might continue for some time. So whilst Mrs Brown was clear about the different levels over which she had to operate in her work with Mrs Simpson, she needed to ensure that Mrs Simpson was clear about her purpose in continuing to see her:

I wanted to enable her to feel that I was someone, without a specific role in her life, who was not going to do anything in particular for her, but who could sit with her; I was not afraid, and could actually listen, whatever she might bring out. If she was not feeling too well, I just sat quietly and held her hand; we did not need to talk.

Mrs Brown also recognised the boundaries of her function. We have already seen that she did not push Mr Simpson beyond his wishes in the expression of his feelings. Nor did she see their children at any time. Mr and Mrs Simpson were both defensive about their children and did not want them to know about the terminal nature of the illness, and Mrs Brown respected their wishes. The social worker never saw Mr and Mrs Simpson together because he avoided this. Only rarely did he see his wife on his own and Mrs Brown had to work hard to get them alone together, as part of her goal-setting plan—to help them to communicate about their situation. One way in which she was able to facilitate this was by arranging with the terminal care unit for Mrs Simpson to have a single room, so that she and her husband could be together. She explained her reason and that it was not because they did not want her to meet people or because she was terribly ill.

Mrs Brown recognised that she had to go at the client's pace:

In some ways I regret that I never saw the two of them together. But on the other hand, I am not sure how far it might have been damaging to try to help them communicate more. They were already having to cope with a great deal of grief and not coping terribly well; had he been pushed that little bit further, I think it might have been more uncomfortable for both of them. As it was, they became very close towards the end. Who was I to change their past communicating patterns at this point!

Mrs Brown was clear herself about the importance of not fracturing the assessment and intervention stages of her work. As we have outlined, she used the waiting time in a positive way, to share anxieties with Mrs Simpson, to help the couple communicate, to facilitate and plan visits home, to keep the reality of the terminal illness in focus and to recognise the boundaries of her role. As she explained:

When I had completed the assessment, before Mrs Simpson moved, it would have been wrong to wait until she was moved and then to begin my interventive work. Therefore, I saw her almost daily before she went. In a sense, by the time she got to the terminal care unit, most of the work had been done. She talked quite a lot and as things got tougher she began to get worried. She sometimes wanted to go over again the fact that she was afraid of being a coward, especially if she had had a bad night and been in a lot of pain. I also had to help her to come to accept the pain control procedures, because at first she refused to take drugs and was not asking for them before she was in pain, when it was controllable. I also did some work to assure the husband that he would manage all right if she went home for an afternoon; he was scared of her dying with him. He then enjoyed being with his wife without feeling unsafe. She went home twice for weekends, and when she returned on the last Monday, she said to me, 'I am now ready to die, thank you very much, and if I do not see you again it is all right; I have said goodbye'. It was happy and complete for her. She died very soon after that. I saw the husband when she had just died and he agreed that the last weekend had been very good. The ward staff had told me that his wife was ready to die.

The conclusion to the work is best described in Mrs Brown's own words:

The outstanding thing I remember from this case was their tremendous honesty and openness throughout and that I learned a great deal from Mrs Simpson. I felt that it was a very satisfactory piece of work because here was a woman who potentially, when I first saw her, was going to die in a great deal of physical and emotional stress—in a fantasy rather than honest world. In the event, she died what I would call a very good death, having been able to go home for a time, and return able to say, 'I am now ready to die, I have done all those things outstanding and it is all right now'. It was a very whole piece of work, because in a sense it was working through emotionally and helping her to come to terms with and to face up to the points she wanted to face and tidy up the ends she wanted to tidy up. And for him, perhaps because it had been honest, grieving afterwards was easier.

Part II Analysis

We shall now present an analysis of these three social work assessments; generalisations will be drawn from each case in turn, based on the frameworks which have been employed in the previous four chapters: communication processes in the acquisition of information, frameworks for studying facts and feelings, balance sheets in formulating assessments, strategies in setting goals, assessment and intervention processes.

Each case is open to different interpretations, according to the assumptions or theory which are used to analyse it. For example, John Prince's behaviour could be interpreted as an expression of family tensions from a psycho-dynamic perspective; the ward culture in situations of terminal illness rather than the Simpsons' emotional and social needs might have been the target for intervention from a systems approach (Foster, 1973); the political economy of welfare in non-accidental injury cases might have led to a very different assessment of the Jones's referral. As the cases are presented in quite a lot of detail, readers are invited to make alternative interpretations of them. However, our purpose is to document practice theories by using a specific and selected framework which is based on the particular model of assessment processes which has been used in this book.

Acquisition of information

There were many things about these three cases which created potential difficulties for the social workers as they gathered their information: a possible prosecution for non-accidental injury in the baby Jones's case; John Prince's reception into care or transfer to a school for maladjusted children; in the case of Mrs Simpson, a woman who was going to die in circumstances as emotionally painful for herself as they would be for her husband. There was some evidence that the social workers were able to acquire adequate and relevant information on the basis of which they could make a competent assessment. Their work was founded on principles of social work practice as well as on knowledge from social science and social work theory and we shall explore some of the ways in which these facilitated their assessments.

Preparation

The social workers had preliminary information before they went to their first interviews with their respective clients, but they gathered and used it in different ways. Miss Bell's first response was to delay her first interview with the baby's parents whilst she contacted a number of people in a variety of agencies: doctors, child abuse centre, record clerk, health visitor, the baby and nurses; even at this stage information was not gathered in a mechanical way, because appropriate questions were asked of the different informants, and the various accounts were compared. this enabled the social worker to write down some warning signs before she saw the parents. In John Prince's case, the workers visited the home as soon as possible in order to check that the mother's definition of the problem was the same as the one which the local authority social worker had reported: 'disruptive' and 'bizarre' behaviour. Similarly, Mrs Brown visited Mrs Simpson on the ward as soon as she could in order to explore the home situation and the need for practical help on discharge.

Even though the timing of the respective visits differed, the central client was always the primary source of information: Miss Bell saw the young parents before the grandparents; John Prince's parents were contacted before his schoolteachers; Mrs Simpson was seen before her husband.

The purpose of these interviews was made clear to the clients from the onset. Miss Bell explained her involvement to the anxious and bewildered parents, by describing some of the non-accidental injury cases which had been reported in the press, and explaining the meaning of the place of safety order, and what would happen next, such as the blood test and further exploration of the bruising. The university workers made the purpose of their work quite clear to John Prince's parents; they had accepted the referral for assessment and would make several visits to the home in order to complete their task, which would include psychometric tests and observation exercises. The purpose of the assessment was to define and explain the nature of John's behavioural difficulties with a view to planning intervention which would involve the parents. At her first interview with Mrs Simpson, Mrs Brown explained that she saw all ready-for-home patients as a courtesy measure: this is particularly important because Mrs Simpson was 'very prickly' and felt it 'a bit of an insult' that a social worker had gone to see her. Assessment work will get off to a bad start if social workers fail to make clear to the clients from the outset the purpose of their visits. Even so, communication in these circumstances requires particular skills.

Communication

Miss Bell shared with Mrs Jones the information she had about the blood test before she explored further facts and feelings about the situation; she then explained that this meant either that the child had had an accident or that someone had smacked him; in view of the baby's age and vulnerability and their lack of knowledge on which to base a decision, she would apply to the court for a place of safety order. Miss Bell followed up this devastating news by going home with the mother to tell the same story to the father. She found a very difficult situation there in which to communicate with the parents, especially because of the presence and aggression of the grandparents. She managed that interview by separating the grandparents and parents, and interviewing each pair in turn, repeating once again the focus and purpose of the inquiry. Her social work role helped her here because she remained authoritative and clear about her task.

In the case of John Prince, the focus of the assessment was rather different. The workers not only clarified with John's parents the purpose of their visits, they also actively involved them in the assessment by asking the mother to record the times and rates of his behaviours and to identify two major problem categories. The whole context of communication indicated that the workers were called in as experts, who had a particular method in relation to a specific problem-definition. There were hints that communication might have been very different had not the workers accepted the parents' wishes that their marriage and the father's imprisonment were not the problems for which they were currently seeking help. As it was, open communication seemed to be possible because of the context and method of the assessment.

When Mrs Brown saw Mrs Simpson on the ward, she hypothesised that things were not as simple as the referral had indicated, but she kept these thoughts to herself until the situation had been more fully explored. Mrs Simpson did not seem to know how ill she was, and the family might have problems in coping if she were discharged. Further information was needed, so Mrs Brown asked Mrs Simpson if she could see her husband. She needed to find out how much he knew about the medical prognosis and to assess his coping abilities before his feelings about the situation were sought. The social worker's interviewing and communication skills were evident in the way in which she managed, timed and paced her interviews with the relevant parties; she never saw Mr and Mrs Simpson together because they did not want this. She arranged for Mr Simpson to see the doctor so that he would have relevant information about his wife's condition before his feelings about discharge were sought. Mrs Brown clarified with Mrs Simpson both her role (enabler) and information about the resources she could arrange, such as the pain control and the weekends home.

Barriers to communication

There are many reasons why barriers to communication arise during assessment interviews, as these three cases illustrate. The worker might anticipate some blocks to communication, as when Miss Bell anticipated that the family of the bruised baby might be 'anti-welfare' from the outset, and Mrs Brown thought that Mrs Simpson might block out the emotional implications of her illness. These difficulties are compounded if social workers inappropriately label their clients on the basis of their class and cultural background. Miss Bell had to identify, then work with and through the 'anti-welfare' attitudes of the baby's grandparents, who were creating barriers to communication. Mrs Brown had to walk a tightrope between respecting the wishes of a middle-class couple and appropriately reaching out to them to meet their emotional needs.

Another way in which clients may create barriers to communication is by trying to deflect the worker from the purpose of the inquiry. The baby Jones's relatives constantly tried to turn the discussion to other matters than the actual bruises, and there was enough evidence of 'need' to tempt Miss Bell in this respect. It could be speculated that John Prince's parents blocked communication by refusing to discuss their marriage and criminality; the workers were aware of this, but decided that their focus should be on the boy's behaviour. Even so, the temptation to change John's behaviour might have led them towards a faulty assessment in the family.

There are degrees of blocking in interview situations and sometimes the diffulty arises from normal anxiety; for example, it was a normal reaction for Mr Simpson to become tense, rigid and silent when the doctor gave him the news about his wife's condition. It was also understandable that he vacillated between wanting to take his wife home and requesting her transfer to the terminal care unit. Social workers must be sensitive to and understanding about such reactions in order to respond appropriately.

Communication may also be blocked because clients obtain gratification from their problems. Perhaps the Princes got satisfaction from John's behavioural difficulties. As the mother said, she would not wish his comic role to be conditioned away; so the workers had to assess with care whether or not John's mother was getting gratification from either his buffoon rôle or his behavioural difficulties.

Overcoming communication barriers

It is understandable why there were barriers to communication in each of these cases: the welfare were visiting over such a private matter as a young baby; a couple's personal difficulties were open to examination because of the visibility of their son's behavioural problems; a middle class family's vulnerability was being exposed because the wife was terminally ill. Even so, it is not enough for social workers to identify or understand such blocks as 'anti-welfare' attitudes, 'presenting symptoms' and 'prickliness'; they must also find ways of overcoming some of these blocks in order to complete a satisfactory assessment.

Social workers need to create an enabling atmosphere which both facilitates and protects the ability of their clients to share facts and feelings about a situation. For example, Miss Bell met a lot of aggression from the baby's grandmothers; as each in turn 'tore her off a strip', she 'had to stay with the fact of a child with bruises' and remain with and work through their aggression. There were obvious blocks to communication in this case, given the discrepancies in the explanations about the bruising which the parents were offering to different people. Miss Bell overcame these barriers in a variety of ways. For example, she reached out to those young parents in their distress by putting her arms round the mother; she interviewed the parents and the grandparents separately; and—the hardest of all—she 'stayed with the fact of the bruises' when efforts were being made to deflect her to make a pleasant but less appropriate

147

relationship. She relied on the strength of her personality as well as on her techniques in these difficult situations.

The workers in the case of John Prince faced different communication issues. As experts in behavioural casework, they worked with authority in their methods; communication blocks were overcome by actively involving the parents in the assessment process. It could be argued that they did not successfully overcome the blocks to communication which the parents were presenting in relation to their own marital difficulties, but the workers quite consciously (and on theoretical and methodological grounds) took the parents' request about John's behaviour seriously and chose not to explore the family dynamics from a psycho-social perspective.

Mrs Brown met several barriers to communication in her work with the Simpsons: Mrs Simpson's prickliness, her husband's vacillations, and their own personal and cultural styles about public display of feelings. Some of these barriers had to be accepted and respected, but others had to be overcome and worked with if appropriate help was going to be provided. Mrs Brown created an enabling atmosphere as she sat with and explored Mrs Simpson's knowledge and feelings about her situation: 'I sat with her, was not afraid, and could actually listen, whatever she might bring out. I sat quietly and held her hand—we did not need to talk'. When Mrs Brown stayed with Mr Simpson following the interview in which the doctor had told him about his wife's condition, she knew that she had to 'hang on at all costs' because it was a natural immediate reaction for him to want to withdraw himself and his wife from the situation. Mrs Brown had to 'hang on' because she was not sure that they could cope without social work support. She always went at the clients' pace, and limited and facilitated information sought and given at any one time. For example, she shared with them the various options available, and allowed them to think about them before she explored their feelings further. Mrs Brown respected the wishes of Mr and Mrs Simpson and kept confidences.

Many barriers to communication can be appropriately overcome if social workers manage to create an enabling atmosphere, limit and facilitate information, maintain confidentiality and use themselves in the relationship.

Studying facts and feelings

These social workers were engaged in a complex process of study rather than an *ad hoc* collection of facts. The boundaries of their study were related to the nature of the referral (= offence), the circumstances of the clients (= offender) and the settings (= social control) in which their work was conducted.

Relevance of frameworks

The referral

The focus of study in the case of the Jones baby was the bruising; though Miss Bell had to 'stay with the fact of the bruises', she explored the meaning of it as she studied the situation. Eventually, and on well-thought-out grounds, she decided that the seriousness of and responsibility for the bruising was less important than the 'background of these young and vulnerable parents with such a messy looking extended family' and began to think of changes needed in their situation so that injury would be less likely to recur. She dealt with the referral issue in an individualised way rather than on the tariff. The history of the family was studied in a similar way.

The workers studied the seriousness of John Princes's behaviour by using a specific formula (FINDS) to examine the frequency, intensity, number, duration and sense of the behaviour. Whilst they were able to measure the behaviours in a very precise way, the sense of them was thought to be more important than their seriousness. The behaviour was studied in terms of its individualised meaning, given the social circumstances in which it occured. Similarly, John's history was considered in careful detail, but given meaning in terms of his current circumstances. Individualisation rather than seriousness was the key to the study in this case too.

From the outset, Mrs Brown was thinking of the practical and emotional implications of Mrs Simpson's illness rather than the fact of the cancer (= tariff) *per se*. To the extent that her history was relevant, it was studied in terms of Mrs Simpson's reactions to suffering from a condition from which both her mother and her sister had previously died.

The referral issues were taken seriously, but explored in terms of their individual meaning for the clients and the people surrounding them. The workers acknowledged the seriousness of the referral problems but explored them rather than just accepting their official definitions.

The clients' circumstances

Strengths and stresses in the clients' situation were carefully studied.

Miss Bell concluded that there were more stresses than strengths in the situation; there was reason for concern about the clients' personal family, economic, neighbourhood, health and social situation, which indicated high social stress.

The balance was rather different in the case of John Prince. The social worker who referred the case commented on the strengths in the situation, including the mother's positive concern about and

149

coping abilities in relation to John. The workers also carefully studied John's pro-social behaviour. This led them to the conclusion that John was not all 'problem' but there were aspects of his specific behaviour which had profound ramifications for himself, his family, his school, and his friends.

The relevance of frameworks for study is less easily identifiable in the case of Mrs Simpson; this was a classic situation in which surface strengths belied underlying emotional and social weaknesses. Mrs Brown concluded that the couple would have problems if Mrs Simpson were discharged home, even though there were many strengths evident in the situation.

The idea of strengths and stresses oversimplifies the way the social workers studied these cases, but it does help us to identify one way in which the need for social work intervention is identified at the study stage of the assessment process.

Settings

The referral problem and the clients' needs must always be studied in the context of agency function and resources. Miss Bell had neither to give in to nor bargain with her agency and the court in the non-accidental injury inquiry. But she had to use them appropriately, and, interestingly, she found the clear-cut formalised procedures a positive support. They helped her to handle the stressful emotions as well as the specific tasks which were necessary in that painful situation. Similarly, she felt helped by the fact that it was the case conference and the court which had the responsibility for the final decision; it was her responsibility to make as good an assessment as she could. Social control factors such as agency function and court policy can therefore be a positive aid to the social worker, even though sometimes they may be felt to be restricting.

The social control factors were rather different in the case of John Prince. The university unit was a voluntary agency with no statutory functions, so the workers were free to take on whichever clients they thought most suitable to their way of working. Even so, they had to study whether their resources could handle the referral for assessment, and to decide whether they would have to work with other professionals in order to complete their task. They decided not to negotiate with the education authorities and school psychological service, but to confine their study to the family and school setting. This had important implications for the kind of assessment they made and their future intervention.

Social control factors were very helpful to Mrs Brown as she studied the Simpsons' situation. First, she had a responsibility, given her role in the hospital, to assess the Simpsons' emotional and social needs. Second, she had co-operative relationships with the hospital staff who were willing to delay Mrs Simpson's discharge until an appropriate assessment and relevant arrangements had been made. Third, there was the resource of the terminal care unit, with which Mrs Brown could negotiate in order to facilitate her assessment plans. Hospital social workers are not always blessed with such relationships and resources.

The study stage of any assessment involves a constant weighing of factors. How serious is the referral and what does it mean? Do social control networks and resources have to be accepted or bargained with? Do stresses outweigh strengths in the clients' situation? These frameworks were evident in the work of the social workers in these three cases, and provide useful guidelines for practice.

Frameworks for study

Explicit theories of practice are one means by which cases can be studied in a systematic way. There was evidence that these social workers were drawing on explicit theories in a systematic way in these assessments. Miss Bell used her knowledge from social science and social work theory and methods in her assessment of the Jones family. There was evidence that she used her knowledge about child health, sociology and psychology in relation to the baby and his interactions with his mother in their family, community and cultural context. She drew on knowledge about how people are likely to react in emotional situations. She used her knowledge about the agency's procedures and resources, and she was aware of current and future legislation and used this appropriately. Miss Bell's knowledge helped her to make some sense of an extremely complex situation and to act appropriately within it.

The knowledge base of the workers was very evident in the case of John Prince. They explicitly, systematically and rigorously drew on learning theory in order to assess the nature and meaning of John's behaviour which was defined as a problem. The formulae they used for this were drawn from behavioural psychology:

FINDS — Frequency, Intensity, Number, Duration and Sense of the Behaviour

ABC — Antecedents, Behaviour and Consequences

They also used their knowledge about interviewing and communication, cultural and social contexts and social policies, but their over-riding framework was learning theory.

It was clear that Mrs Brown had expert knowledge about the nature of terminal illness, the needs of people and the special aspects of communication in these situations:

One of the particular difficulties with terminal care is that every interview has to be absolute and complete in itself. At the end of the interview you have to have covered and taken in a lot of the feelings and emotions and be able to bring it up to a positive, hopeful ending, because they may well die. On the other hand, you have got to have some sort of ongoing plan of work to be doing.

Such knowledge is much more than common sense or hunch; it might have been internalised or tested out against experience, but it also springs from social science and social work methods knowledge. All social workers draw on many sources of knowledge, and most social workers will typically resort to particular ranges of knowledge at the expense of others. Either way, a specific knowledge base is indispensable in social work assessments.

Ideologies are another indispensable framework for study. When we described the practices of probation officers, we were able to refer to 'treatment' and 'non-treatment' ideologies respectively. We did not systematically explore ideologies in these three cases. (For example, we could have tried to identify whether the social workers employed a justice, welfare or community ideology; Parsloe, 1976, Smith, 1977). It did seem that some kind of treatment/welfare ideology was the conclusion to the study in each case. Miss Bell did not agree that the bruising was a symptom of the family's underlying personal problems to the extent that the family 'deliberately bruised the baby so that their problems would come to light'. But she concluded that there were other problems in the family, which was how the problems had come to light (presenting *symptom*). She explained the bruising in terms of the family's *background*, and thought about their emotional and social *needs*. She explained the bruising in terms of its context and decided that it was not either a chance, isolated or freely-chosen action. This explanation led her to think in terms of the need for intervention—she used a treatment ideology in coming to the conclusion of her study.

The behavioural caseworkers insisted on using specific rather than global methods and measurements as they studied John's behaviour. Clearly, a treatment ideology was implicit in their approach. They explained John's behaviour in terms of his background, thought that his actions were more problematical than other children's and that the parents' request was a pointer to the need for social work intervention. They concluded that the problems were related to the situation, rather than isolated or freely-chosen behaviours, and that intervention would be appropriate.

Mrs Brown also related Mrs Simpson's needs to her situation; the patient was not aware that she was dying and neither she nor her husband was realistic about how they would be able to cope if she was discharged home. Their feelings could be explained in terms of their background but it was their middle-class culture, networks and socialisation rather than their lack of intelligence, or emotional or social deprivation, which influenced their 'coping styles'. They were in 'need' in their current, painful situation.

This discussion of social work ideologies has been rather unsatisfactory, because we have had to speculate rather a lot. Even so, it did seem that the underlying attitude of these social workers indicated that they thought that their clients' needs were related to their personal and social situation, and that social work intervention seemed to be appropriate.

Formulating an Assessment

Social workers draw up a balance sheet as they formulate their assessments, and, in respect of probation officers, we described this as a 'reverse tariff'. In other kinds of social work, the equation seems to consist of estimations of risk, need and resource. These exactly parallel the frameworks we outlined for the study stage of assessments:

'risk' relates to the referral issue;
'need' summarises the client's circumstances;
'resources' refer to settings.

The formulation which Miss Bell reached was that the parents were able to accept her support and intervention and could use social work help in spite of their elusiveness. However, their acceptance of intervention could not be taken for granted, because the parents' co-operation could not be guaranteed without the sanction of a care order, and the grandparents might sabotage a supervision order. These possibilities had to be carefully weighed, because the moderate risk of sending the baby home had to be balanced against the grave risk that, if he were brought into care of the local authority at his age, he would be likely to stay there for many years. The parents' needs had also to be considered and the social worker thought that the overriding task here was 'the need for somebody to help them to strengthen the adult bit of them'. The moderate risk and the high need seemed to be manageable if the baby went home on a care order, because appropriate agency resources could be mobilised. If the risk had been greater or fewer resources had been available, Miss Bell would have had seriously to consider taking the baby into long-term care. The balance sheet was quite complex but precise in this case.

The formulation took a rather different form in the case of John Prince. If nothing were done, there was the risk that he would become labelled maladjusted and/or subnormal and removed to a school for maladjusted children. John was not at risk in his family, but his mother was asking for specific help to control her son. The need related to making life more pleasant for the family and also enhancing John's personal development. Resources had to be considered in relation to the risk of non-intervention, and the mother's request for specific help. But the family's resources had to be considered in addition to the help the unit could offer. Were the parents sufficiently resourceful to co-operate in a behavioural programme with John? In this case, the balance sheet indicated that family and agency resources were sufficient to handle the specific requests for help, especially since non-intervention might have unfortunate consequences.

Mrs Brown went through two separate formulation stages in her work with the Simpsons. The risk in the situation was acknowledged, because Mrs Simpson was terminally ill and nothing could change that 'reality' factor. So the balance sheet hinged on the identification of needs in relation to available resources. First, Mrs Brown had written off the possibility of Mrs Simpson being discharged home, because the couple had neither the practical nor the emotional resources to cope with the situation of terminal illness. However, there were resources for other lines of action, and Mrs Simpson was not just left to die in the hospital. Second, Mrs Brown identified the Simpsons' needs in relation to their own feelings about the situation and the resources which could be mobilised in the terminal care unit. The formulation was that resources were available in relation to the Simpsons.

These cases illustrate how important it is for social workers to draw up a balance sheet as they make their assessments, because the factors in the situation have to be given some weighting. If the Jones' baby had been very severely injured, or if John's parents had been overwhelmed by his behaviour, or if there had been no terminal care unit to which Mrs Simpson could go, the formulations reached would have been very different. This would also have had important implications for the goals which were set.

Goal-setting

The social workers had to include other agencies as a party to their goal-setting: the *court* in the non-accidental injury referral, the *school* which John Prince was attending and the *hospitals* caring for Mrs Simpson. It had been agreed at the formulation stage that some kind of intervention was appropriate, so the social workers had to start setting goals accordingly. They made some recommendations as a means of doing this; for example, Miss Bell recommended a care order to the court, and Mrs Brown asked the ward sister to delay Mrs Simpson's discharge; the workers in the university unit decided not to ask the education authorities to delay John's transfer to a school for maladjusted children. These recommendations were not the goals, but a means of setting more complex goals.

Goals

Miss Bell was very clear that her immediate goal was to make a good assessment in order to comply with her agency's procedures, and the goals she set indicated the need for social work intervention. She had to set interim goals, though, in order to conduct her assessment. For example, she had to apply for a place of safety order and to arrange foster-care for the baby. She also had to set some immediate goals for the parents as, 'they had to feel that they were doing something that was likely to have an effect, otherwise they would have just lapsed into total apathy and depression'. This was why the worker made contracts with them about seeing her and visiting the baby. An additional complication was Miss Bell's role in the intake team because she had to decide at what stage she would hand over the case to the long-term worker. But all these goals were related to the assessment at this stage; whatever goals might be agreed when long-term intervention began, the immediate task was to set assessment goals.

The goal which was set at the conclusion of the assessment of John Prince was that the university unit workers could intervene to try to alter the interaction between John and his parents and to change some of the interactions at his school. These goals of establishing self-control and environmental controls were set in rather broad terms at this stage; they would be operationalised in more specific ways once the intervention proper started. The goals were shared with John and his parents and some agreements were made at this goal-setting stage.

Mrs Brown went throught two goal-setting stages in relation to the two assessments she had formulated. First, when she had ruled out the possibility of Mrs Simpson being discharged home, she decided there was little which could be provided physically that the family did not already have, that Mrs Simpson probably could not cope at home, and that more had to be found out about the family's emotional and social coping abilities. The goal at this stage was to establish whether they wanted her to die at home. Second, when Mrs Brown had formulated her plan of intervention in relation to the terminal care, her goals were to help Mr and Mrs Simpson to communicate between themselves about the situation; to enable Mrs Simpson to return home if possible, and to offer emotional support to each individually to talk through the trauma. Part of her task at this stage was to discuss with the ward staff the fact that she had made the decision that Mrs Simpson should not go home for several reasons, which meant that a hospital bed was going to be blocked. Mrs Brown shared her plans with the Simpsons as she went along, and they were all agreed on the future course of action.

Strategies

These social workers' goal-setting strategies differed in interesting ways. Miss Bell had to present a report to the case conference, where a decision would be made about the appropriate course of action; then a court report was prepared, which outlined the assessment which had been reached and the reasons behind the recommendation for the care order. The university unit workers were not required to present a report to another agency; the local authority social worker who referred the case agreed to their decision to intervene at the conclusion of the assessment stage; a report was not sent to the school psychological service and education authorities who had the power to transfer John to the school for maladjusted children. Mrs Brown had to present her assessment to the ward staff, who were willing to keep Mrs Simpson until a bed became vacant in the terminal care unit. These cases bring out very clearly the ways in which goal-setting related to the assessment rather than the intervention stage of the social work process.

Assessment and intervention

However analytically distinct the assessment and intervention phases of work are, the cases illustrate that the phases do not occur in a neat, cut-and-dried sequence. First, even within the assessment phase, the stages overlap. Miss Bell was studying her information as she acquired it and was formulating her assessment as she studied the interactions between the mother and baby in the foster-home. Second, intervention occurred during the assessment phase. There was no need for practical resources to be mobilised immediately in any of these cases, but the workers obviously engaged in a relationship with their clients. They also intervened in order to complete the assessment. Miss Bell arranged the foster placement and applied for the place of safety order, the university workers began to work with the parents in order to complete their assessment, and Mrs Brown saw Mr Simpson, arranged the interview with the doctor and began negotiations with the terminal care unit as part of her assessment.

Third, intervention actually facilitated the assessment. Miss Bell was able to assess the mother's relationship with the baby as she arranged the foster-care. The university workers were able to assess the parents' motivation and ability to change as they involved them in the behavioural programme. Their very assessment techniques also brought about some change, as when the mother began to anticipate the circumstances which produced John's 'bizarre' behaviour. Mrs Brown was also assessing the emotional coping abilities of the Simpsons during her short-term intervention.

There were differences in the timing and pacing of these three assessments. Miss Bell had to complete her assessment within ten days, whereas the university unit workers knew from the outset that their assessment would be more protracted. Mrs Brown completed her assessment within a short period of time. But these workers could not terminate their work with their clients when they finished their assessment. Each of them was clear about the difference between assessment and intervention, but they had to start their interventions before the action resulting from the assessment occurred. Miss Bell had to negotiate with the housing authorities and to work with the parents during the initial setback. The university workers had to work with John's school. Mrs Brown was actively involved with the terminal care unit, but she also had to work with Mrs Simpson whilst she was waiting to be transferred to the terminal care unit. The assessment/intervention stages were very distinct in the work with John Prince, they merged in Miss Bell's work and they became almost fused towards the end of Mrs Brown's work with the Simpsons. Even so, the workers were clear about the distinct phases of their assessment and intervention in each case.

Conclusion

The assessment process in these cases had many parallels with the work done by John Smith's probation officer. Information was acquired in the context of interpersonal relationships, within which blocks to communication were recognised and overcome. Sense was made of exceedingly complex situations by individualising the referral problems, exploring strengths and stresses in the clients' situations and working with the resources available within the agencies. A treatment ideology seemed to be identifiable in each case, because problems were related to the clients' backgrounds and thought to indicate the need for social work intervention. The social workers drew on many sources and frameworks of knowledge to assist them in these assessments. But they were also able to weight their knowledge, as they balanced risks, needs and resources during the formulation stage. It was on this basis that they each decided that social work intervention was indicated. They had to engage in various strategies in order to set these goals, depending on the different settings within which their assessments were made. In each case, it seemed to be appropriate to make analytical distinctions between the assessment and intervention stages of their work. The workers could not rely on their theories of practice alone. However much knowledge they had about criminal behaviour, non-accidental injury, behavioural problems or terminal illness, the workers had to rely on their own feelings and observations in order to come to a comprehensive and integrated conclusion about exceedingly complex situations. It is their practice theories which have been drawn out, documented and analysed in this chapter.

Chapter seven

Conclusion

We suggested in the opening chapter that Mr Smith's probation officer relied on both his textbook knowledge and his experience in order to marshal data for his social inquiry. The rest of this book has been a kind of journey, in which we have explored some of the ways in which social workers use different types and sources of knowledge as they make their assessments. This has been done in the belief that social workers use knowledge much more systematically than is generally recognised. Unfortunately, much of this knowledge remains implicit in social work practice because it is rarely written down. This is one reason why social workers frequently refer to their 'practice wisdom' rather than to their use of 'theory' when they are describing to others their work with clients. Because this has had the unfortunate result that social workers often see 'theory' and 'practice' as opposites, we found it quite useful to think instead in terms of 'theories of practice' and 'practice theories'. The first term refers to knowledge which is borrowed in a relatively unmodified form from the social sciences; the other indicates the implicit knowledge base of social work practice which is rarely codified as discrete 'theory' as such.

It is one thing to *believe* that social workers use knowledge in a systematic way and to talk in terms of their implicit practice theories; it is quite another thing to demonstrate how they use their implicit knowledge systematically. We think that, to an extent, we have successfully identified and used one method in this book to explore social workers' practice theories. The stages in this process of analysis have been as follows:

1　A systematic sample of probation officers' social inquiry reports and interview transcripts was available to us. (Hardiker, 1975; 1977b).

2   Haines's model of assessment processes (1975) was found to be a useful means of identifying some of the activities in which probation officers were engaged during their social inquiry work.
3   The same model was found to be relevant to our exploration of assessment processes in other social work settings (Chapter six).
4   Some generalisations were made about social work practice in a variety of assessment situations. Whilst there is statistical evidence elsewhere to support most of these generalisations (Hardiker, 1975; 1977a; 1977b; 1978; Hardiker and Webb, 1978), their relevance to 'practice theory' could only be understood through examining them in the context of what social work conventionally regards as its theory and methods. For example, 'tariff' is a social science concept about which there is some statistical evidence, but we also had to think about it in social work terms in order to understand some of the ways in which practitioners perceive the seriousness of the referral problem in their social inquiry work.

As we have moved from the case of John Smith to examine a larger sample of social inquiry assessments, we have been 'unpacking' some of the constituent elements in the tasks social workers habitually fulfil. It is unlikely that practitioners themselves reflect for one moment on all the items which we have identified as being essential elements in the assessment process. Even so, they frequently rely on some of their own rules or signposts to help them to make sense of exceedingly complex situations and to come to some decision about appropriate action. It is these rules and signposts which we have been trying to 'identify' in this book, because we wanted to find out how social workers actually make assessments rather than to provide prescriptions for practice (Forder and Kay, 1973).

We think that 'practice theories' are an assemblage of signposts which social workers have accumulated in the course of their work. These signposts are made up of a combination of explicit theoretical knowledge, practice wisdom, experience, feelings and observations. But the *process* by which all these ingredients are employed is little understood and it might be useful to think provisionally in terms of a cartographical analogy for a moment. Lone explorers in earlier generations did not even have maps to outline the boundaries of continents, let alone the nature of a country's interior. They had to work out their own rules and signposts during their voyages. Modern travellers, on the other hand, have maps to guide them in their journeys, which speed their progress and help them to avoid the vicissitudes of unmapped territory; maps also help to avoid the swamps! Social workers are frequently in the situation of having to reconnoitre, mapping out territories and building bridges and signposts in a complex world. But one of the problems is that these signposts are rarely documented, so that each generation of social workers has to work out many of its own practice rules for itself. There will always be an element of individual-working-out in social work practice, particularly because human beings are even more complex than jungles, rivers and mountains. However, it may be possible to identify and document some of these signposts, which can then be taught relatively explicitly to future generations of social workers.

So, we shall now attempt to summarise some 'directional indicators' for social work assessments, and in so doing we shall discuss practice in terms of models, theories and paradigms.

Models

We have examined at least ninety probation officers' social inquiry reports in our work for this book. These reports plus the transcripts of interviews with the probation officers who wrote them amounted to an immense amount of information which we had to learn how to handle. One method of handling a mass of data is to use models, which list the elements to be covered in a particular field. For example, psychologists use models of personality, which would include elements such as feelings, behaviour, perceptions and self-concepts, the purpose being to explore some aspects of human nature. Likewise, we used a model to grapple with the complexities of assessment and, which was made up of elements from Haines's framework (1975) combined with some of our own observations about social inquiry assessments.

It will be apparent to those familiar with this area that this scheme over simplifies the complexity and richness of assessment processes in social inquiries, However, models themselves do not stand as either true or false, but rather, more or less useful for a particular purpose.

So, whilst we can acknowledge that models necessarily oversimplify particular situations, they may help us to organise our data and to identify some of the major aspects of complex situations. Models are, therefore, not only useful, they are also indispensable for some purposes. For example, there is no way in which we could have presented every piece of evidence which was available to us about ninety social inquiry assessments. Even the detailed presentations of the three cases in Chapter six included only selections from a mass of evidence which we had collected from the social workers. On the

161

Conclusion

Model of Assessment Processes

Haines	*Curnock and Hardiker*
Acquisition of information	frameworks
	settings
	communication boundaries
	communication barriers
Studying facts and feelings	frameworks:
	offence/referral problem
	offender/client situation
	social control/settings
	relevance of frameworks
Formulation	risk
	need
	resource
Goal-setting	recommendations
	need for intervention
	contracting
	reports
	strategies
∗ Assessment and intervention	phases
	purposes

other hand, without a model to provide a framework for our analysis, we would have had to present *ad hoc* illustrations from which few generalisations could have been drawn. So models have advantages and disadvantages (they may distort reality to an unwarranted degree), but they are indispensable for handling a mass of data and for helping in generalising from specific and discrete situations.

If we return to our cartographical analogy once more, models are a means of mapping out the boundaries and contours of continents. We have ourselves been mapping out the boundaries of assessment processes, the elements of which are outlined in the diagram presented above. The constituent elements in this model are: acquisition, study, formulation, goal-setting and assessment/intervention phases. These elements are made up of such things as frameworks, communication, balance sheets of risk, need, resource and goal-setting strategies. But travellers require more than contours and boundaries of continents; they need more precise directions to explore pathways through jungles and over mountains. Likewise, social workers need further directions that are not yet evident within this assessment model. How do they get from acquisition to study, or draw up balance sheets, or set goals? How do they know which frameworks are relevant in a particular case, or what strategies to employ in their reports? A model starts them off but it does not help them with their actual journey. For this they need something which will help them to make *connections* between the different parts of the model. Signposts are almost indispensable to travellers; they are useful to social workers, and it is these signposts or theoretical connections which we shall now explore.

Theories

Theories take us a stage further than models in our understanding of social work practice because they begin to provide some explanations of processes. For example, we indicated above that psychologists use models of personality which include elements such as behaviour, feelings and self-concepts. These elements do not themselves provide an explanation of psychological processes; we need to turn to theories for these explanations. Psychologists use different theories to explain the connection between elements such as behaviour and feelings. Behaviourists use theories of learning—such as classical and operant conditioning—to explain how complex repertoires of behaviour are derived, whereas (classical) psychoanalysts explain behaviour in terms of the vicissitudes of instinctual drives as they come into conflict with the reality principle. Similarly, most social workers employ some kind of model which links the person with his situation. But how the person is linked with his situation will be explained in different ways depending on the particular theory which is being used. Some workers rely on role theory to make these connections, whilst others turn to learning processes or unconscious defence mechanisms, in their search for an explanation of how a particular person functions in his situation. All these theories provide signposts to which to connect feelings and behaviour, perceptions and self-concepts, roles and situations. Social workers would find it extremely difficult to assess complex human situations if they did not possess a set of theoretical signposts to make these links. They do just this, though we do not think many others have described the processes involved. We think we have been moving towards the identification of a practice theory as opposed to a practice model as we have explored assessment processes in social inquiries. Not only have we identified and used a model, we have begun to make some connections between the elements within it. These connections can be specified in terms of the following theoretical keys:

1 Interpersonal communication processes.
2 Individualisation within the context of treatment ideologies.
3 Balance sheets of risk, need and resource.

4   Goal-setting strategies.
5   Boundaries of the assessment role in social inquiries.

We shall discuss these theoretical keys in greater detail.

Interpersonal communication processes

Most social workers have experienced problems in collecting even basic facts from their clients, and this is the baseline from which social inquiry work begins. But the preparation of a report for another agency or colleague is more than a simple fact-finding exercise and involves the social worker in a complex process of interpersonal communication, usually within the context of an interview. Social workers have developed some guidelines which have proved to be helpful and relevant in these circumstances. For example, careful preparation for the setting and purpose of the interview has been found to ease the tensions of the first meeting. Anticipating how the client will be likely to react to the inquiry also seems to help the social worker to pitch and pace his questions. Understanding some of the typical reasons why clients block communication may also be halfway towards overcoming such barriers, especially if social workers understand that people are playing specific roles in social inquiry interviews.

All these signposts have been traditionally heard of in the 'practice wisdom' of social work. We have been exploring their relevance to the acquisition stage of our assessment model. But it is very interesting that some of these 'homespun' rules, which social workers have developed for themselves, have also been codified, in symbolic interaction theory (Manis and Meltzer, 1967; Mead, 1934; Rose, 1962). For example, human interaction relies on the ability of the participants to 'take roles' and this can only happen if they anticipate each other's likely reactions and monitor their own responses accordingly. Because human beings have a symbolic language, they can think before they act; they do not respond to each other like billiard balls but construct their behaviour in relation to their understanding of what is happening in a particular situation.

If we are making theoretical connections about the process of collecting information by specifying rules and dynamics about communication processes during the acquisition stage, what is the nature of the theory we are using? We can rule out psycho-dynamic theory, because we would then give more weight to unconscious rather than symbolic processes. Neither is it systems theory, because the client would not then necessarily be the primary source of information. Nor is it learning theory, because more weight would then be given to the identification of reinforcements for behaviour through the use of specific assessment techniques. We would have to plump for the term psycho-social theory as this comes nearest to our own approach.

Thus, a combination of 'practice wisdom' and symbolic interaction theory helps social workers—albeit implicitly—to make some connections between the person-in-his-situation (Hollis, 1972; Rein, 1970a, 1970b; Evans and Webb, 1977, 1978). This means that social workers try to make sense of both their client's life-situation and the things that are happening during an interview by thinking in terms of people's needs in the context of their social situation; some offenders do steal from their employers because they are hungry; family tensions and child-rearing problems are sometimes a product of housing and social stress; the prickliness of some middle-class clients is understandable in terms of how professional people are expected to be able to cope with their own life-situations—even unto death.

The acquisition of information is not a technical, fact-finding exercise in social work. It requires communication skills between people in particular contexts, and these include the skill of making sense of a particular client's problems in relation to his unique personal and social situation. Psycho-social theory seems to be the best way to summarise the combination of 'practice wisdom' and symbolic interaction theory which social workers use in such circumstances, even though much of this knowledge is used implicitly.

Individualisation and treatment ideologies

We have already said that social workers try to make sense of people in particular situations as they gather information for their inquiries and that they have developed certain rules for communication in these circumstances. But, however typical or general a client's situation and problems seem to be, a way has to be found of finding out what they mean to that particular person. Individualisation is the theoretical key which helps us to be rather more specific about this 'making sense' process. Social workers examine the referral issue in each new social inquiry, and either acknowledge its relative seriousness or interpret it as a symptom of the person's problems. They can only come to such a conclusion by individualising the presenting problems (crime, non-accidental injury, illness) in relation to a particular client's life situation, such as strengths and stresses in his personal or social circumstances. Because practitioners are not free-floating observers of the social scene, individualisation is also relevant to the social worker's understanding of the setting in which he is making his assessments. The referral problem and the client's situation have to be studied in relation to the policies and resources of the social work agency and the community. Sometimes, it is concluded that little can be done about a client's problems, whereas in other cases, it is possible to negotiate some kind of intervention.

Individualisation is the key to the study stage. The referral issue, the client's problem and the agency setting are each studied in terms of what they mean for a particular person for whom a social inquiry is being prepared. Whilst individualisation is a controversial value in theory and skill in social work (Statham, 1978), it is a concept which helps us to make sense of some of the processes in which social workers are engaged as they make assessments during their social inquiries.

The concept of ideology is the second theoretical key which we identified in the study element of our assessment model. This helps us to understand some of the ways in which social workers use a coherent framework to individualise their social inquiry assessments. For example, the use of a treatment ideology helps social workers to hypothesise that the referral problem might be a symptom of a client's underlying problems, for which intervention could be appropriate. The concept of treatment ideology does not exhaust our theoretical explanation, because there is evidence that social workers also employ non-treatment ideologies in some of their work (Hardiker, 1977a). The concept helps us to see that social workers are not engaged in an *ad hoc* collection of facts which they study and individualise; they have to make some overall sense of a case, and ideologies are one means by which this can be achieved.

As we have already suggested, social workers filter a mass of data in their social inquiry assessments, because the same situation may tell an infinite number of stories. One way in which practitioners selectively perceive a complex world is by individualising the referral issue in relation to a client's particular situation, within the context of treatment ideologies. The theoretical connections between the study elements in the assessment model are that individualised ideologies are the frameworks which social workers use to link the referral, the client and the agency.

A balance sheet of risks, needs and resources

We found that in many cases social workers thought that intervention was indicated but did not recommend this for a variey of reasons. The theoretical key which helped us to explain this was the idea of a balance sheet, which enabled us to show how social workers weigh relevant factors in a situation. For example, the risk of keeping a client in the community was sometimes too great, and so a custodial sentence rather than probation was considered. In other cases, a client had evident needs, but he was already receiving social work support. The availability of appropriate resources was also a factor determining whether help could be offered. Drawing up a balance sheet which weights risks, needs and resources seems to be a crucial stage in any assessment, because social workers have always to consider 'need' in relation to the referral issue and the resources available. If this stage is missed out during social inquiry work, social workers might find themselves recommending supervision when either the risk does not warrant it or resources are not available to provide such help. Similarly, the balance sheet formula enables a social worker to identify whether he is suggesting intervention too early in a client's career, or appealing for a chance to help someone whom society can hardly tolerate in the community. Formulation is an important element in our assessment model, and we need to understand some of the ways in which this is achieved by drawing up a precise balance sheet which weights risks, needs and resources.

Goal-setting strategies

Social workers have not completed their assessment tasks, even when they have drawn up a balance sheet. The idea of goal-setting strategies is the theoretical key which connects the final set of elements in our assessment model. Whether or not social workers decide that intervention is indicated, given the balance sheet which they have already formulated, they must find an appropriate means of communicating their assessment to the people who asked for the social inquiry in the first place: sentencers, doctors, or colleagues. For example, they must decide what recommendation is the most suitable means of giving expression to their goals; if they think an offender should not go to prison, a variety of sentences can achieve this end; if a family is thought to be in need of support in the care of its children, this can be achieved by means of either a care order or a supervision measure.

Social workers have then to compile their social inquiry reports and to share the contents with the clients concerned, and this is not a straightforward procedure. There is evidence that social workers assume different rôles in their social inquiry assessments, and the contents of their reports only make sense once these rôles are identified. For example, they sometimes stress the judicial aspects of their rôle by writing a custody inevitable/classical justice report; at other times, they emphasise the casework aspect of their assessment task, and present a report which is similar to a plea for the defence. In many cases, social workers adopt a more straightforward advisory role and provide a description of a client's circumstances and a diagnosis and prognosis of his behaviour. The logic of the argument presented in this book leads us to suggest that it is appropriate for social workers to adopt the more straightforward advisory rôle rather than either a classical justice or casework function in their social inquiry work. If they are confident that they have taken into account the 'relevant' factors, are clear about the boundaries of their function in social inquiry work, and have made a competent assessment, then they should be able to communicate their story in a relatively straightforward manner in their report.

Whatever conclusion a social worker comes to during his social inquiry work, he has not completed his assessment tasks until he has presented his report. Certain strategies go with this, such as sharing and contracting with the client, compiling a report and communicating the assessment to the people who asked for it. Goal-setting is not an abstract exercise, and social workers engage in a number of strategies as they complete the final links in the assessment chain.

The boundaries of the assessment role

Our model separates the assessment, intervention and evaluation stages of the social work process. The theoretical keys which we have identified so far have made connections between the elements within the assessment model itself: acquisition, study, formulation and goal-setting. We now need to examine the assessment process overall, in order to explain our reasons for locating social inquiry work within this rather than in other phases of the social work process.

We have insisted throughout this book that social workers must be clear that there are boundaries to their function in social inquiry assessments. This is usually because there is a third party to any work which is done between the social worker and the client; the social inquiry report has usually been requested by sentencers, colleagues, schools and doctors, in order to assist them in a decision which they must make. However strongly a social worker feels about his conclusion or recommendation, this really has to be legitimated by the decision of other people. Courts do not always make care orders requested by social workers, doctors sometimes discharge patients despite a recommendation to the contrary, and sentencers may place someone under supervision even though a probation officer has presented clear arguments against such a disposal. All these possibilities have to be taken into account during the assessment stage of social inquiry work, but practitioners must still be clear about the other people involved in the decision-making process.

Not everyone will agree with the analytical distinctions which we have drawn between assessment, intervention and evaluation, or that social inquiry reports are primarily assessments. As an implicit recognition of this we have pointed out that the issues are not so clear-cut in practice and made several qualifications to our own observations.

The assessment filter

We have tried to explain some of the ways in which social workers selectively perceive and filter a mass of data during the course of their social inquiry work. In order to complete their assessments, they must understand something about interpersonal communication processes and be able to individualise any client's situation. Understandings reached at this stage must be taken a step further by weighting risks, needs and resources in a kind of balance sheet; goal-setting strategies will then relate to these formulations. The overriding purpose of all these activities is the preparation of an assessment for another colleague or agency. The assessment filter can be illustrated diagrammatically

The assessment filter

Request for social inquiry report:
Interpersonal *communication* problems explored
as a possibility
Strengths and stresses *individualised*
in relation to referral, client,
agency
Balance sheet drawn up in
relation to risks, needs,
resources.
Goal-setting *strategies*
Report presented
Assessment proper ends

The stages in this assessment filter are really signposts which social workers may follow in any social inquiry. The signposts in themselves will not be sufficient to help them complete their assessment—they are pointers in the right direction, and they should enable practitioners to avoid the 'swamps' and 'jungles' which exist in all human situations. As social workers follow these directions, they will use 'an amalgam of theory plus experience, expressed in professional skill' (Stevenson, 1978, p. 45). Social workers engage in subtle transactions as they work with their clients, and this is why we have used words like 'practice wisdom' and 'practice theory' to identify these processes.

Conclusion

Social workers will never be able to rely exclusively on theoretical knowledge as they work with their clients. Whilst they may draw on many types of knowledge as they handle different cases, ultimately they must rely on a particular blend of feelings, observations and ideas in order to come to an assessment. The constituent elements in this 'blend' have rarely been identified, let alone documented, and this is one of the things we have been trying to do in this book. We have not exhausted our understanding and explanation of social work assessments, but we have identified some signposts which seem to be relevant to assessment processes in most social inquiry situations. Perhaps the signposts or theoretical keys which we have identified can now be called 'theories of practice', in which case we have helped, 'social workers to conceptualise and codify what they do in practice and to incorporate this into our theory', (Evans, 1976, P. 195). In one sense this book should have carried the title, 'Towards Theories of Practice', because this is what we have been moving towards as we have identified certain theoretical keys. However, we think the book is also about 'practice theory', because we have tried to identify some of the ways in which social workers achieve some integration in their assessment practices; it is the *process* of using many sources and types of evidence within the context of a professional relationship which constitutes practice theory. As we have tried to show, interpersonal communication, individualisation, ideologies, balance sheets and goal-setting strategies are key components of practice theory, during the assessment phase of the social work process.

A postscript on paradigms

Whatever theoretical connections we make between the elements in a model, these theories are always to be found within a particular set of assumptions of a specific scientific discipline (Kuhn, 1970). Leonard (1975) suggests that social workers work within several scientific paradigms, represented by behaviourist, systems, psycho-social and Marxist perspectives, respectively. The idea of paradigms helps us to understand some of the assumptions underlying our work for this book, because our material is open to many different interpretations. This may become apparent if we make a few comparisons between the psycho-social/human sciences paradigm on which we think our work has been based with other paradigms which are available to social workers.

Behaviourists adopt a relatively hard line, physical science approach towards their work. Because we have not worked within this paradigm, we had to engage in some mental gymnastics in our analysis of the case of John Prince in Chapter six. We speculated that perhaps John's parents were blocking communication by refusing to discuss their marital problems, and that maybe the university workers did not successfully overcome these communication barriers in this particular assessment. It is appropriate for us to speculate in this way, given the psycho-social paradigm within which we have worked, but we should not indict the university workers for not doing something which was inappropriate, given the paradigm within which they were explicitly working (Herbert, 1978).

A similar problem arose in our analysis of Mrs Simpson, the terminally ill woman discussed in Chapter six. However good Mrs Brown's assessment was, given the paradigm and assumptions within which she worked, a practitioner operating within a systems framework might have engaged in very different assessment tasks. She might have seen the culture of the ward as a more appropriate focus for her assessment (Foster, 1973). If there had been open communication on the ward about death or dying, patients like Mrs Simpson might have become aware of the nature of their illness long before arrangements were made for their discharge. Mrs Simpson's needs could still have been identified, but the assessment might have hinged on a rather different set of issues.

If social workers operate within Marxist assumptions (Corrigan and Leonard, 1978), they are unlikely to take babies into care whilst they make an assessment of the interior dynamics of an extended family, thereby exposing the young parents' vulnerability. Miss Bell, who made the assessment in the case of baby Jones discussed in Chapter six, was extremely competent and caring as she worked with the various members of the family, and ultimately she decided to return the child to a nuclear family situation. Her work made sense, given the psycho-social assumptions within which she worked. On the other hand, her work could have gone in very different directions. She could have built counter systems such as housing pressure groups and day nurseries; she might have engaged in dialogic relationships and conscientisation processes in order to increase the awareness of the members of the family about their oppressive situation (Leonard, 1975a). Marxist social workers would be unlikely to act as 'agents of the State' by placing babies on risk registers!

Therefore, we would like this book to be understood first in relation to the psycho-social assumptions within which we have worked. Our approach to and understanding of social work might seem rather conservative to some readers. We think we can claim some validity for our observations for three reasons. First, the work we have described is relatively recent, as we collected our data between 1974 and 1977. Second, the social inquiries which we have analysed were typical rather than unique, because they were selected on the basis of systematic sampling procedures (Hardiker, 1975;

1977b). Third, even if the face of social work may be changing, we believe that there are common elements in social work practice and that individualisation is the key here.

We have outlined a model, presented some theoretical connections and identified the paradigm within which we have worked. Perhaps we have moved some way towards the development of theories of practice; but we hope our work has helped us to understand in some small ways the complex filtering processes in which social workers are engaged as they work with clients. Traditionally this has been referred to as 'practice wisdom', but we think that it can make claim to a higher theoretical status than this. This is why we hope we have been moving towards an understanding of 'practice theories' too.

Appendices: I

Interview schedule used in the non-accidental injury case

1 *Can you outline the circumstances of the case* ....
   Probe: referral issue ....
           source of referral ....
           agency function ....

2 *Acquisition of information*
   (a) Source: who interviewed ....
                where...
                when ....
                how often ....
   (b) Factors: which factors from the checklist were relevant:
         (i) Referral issues and circumstances ....
        (ii) Previous record ....
       (iii) Family ....
        (iv) Agency functions and team policy ....
         (v) Clients' personality and attitudes........................
        (vi) Community and neighbourhood ....
       (vii) Sentencing policy of the court ....
      (viii) Economic circumstances of the parents ....
        (ix) Other social factors: work, leisure ....
         (x) Health ....
        (xi) Others: specify..

3 *Studying facts and feelings*
   (a) How did you make sense of the case? ....
   (b) Can you tell me why each of the above factors you selected
       was important? ....
   (c) Were you at this stage already thinking of the possible
       outcome of the case? Please elaborate...........................

4 *Formulation*
  (a) Did you find it difficult to come to a conclusion in this case? ....
  (b) What alternative outcomes were possible?
      (x) for, against..
      (y) for, against..
      (z) for, against..
      etc.
  (c) What swung your decision? ....
      Would you be able to elaborate that in terms of:
          risk ....
          need...
          resources ....
  (d) Can you summarise your formulation ....

5 *Goal-setting*
  We are still at the assessment stage:
  goal-setting re assessment conclusion rather than intervention
  (a) what were your:
          (i) problem-definitions...
          (ii) objectives ....
          (iii) means of achieving objectives re problem defined ......
  (b) Were ideas about sharing and contracting relevant in this case? ....
  (c) What did you do? ....
      (include report, case conference, recommendation)

6 *Additional comments*...

Note The structure of the interview schedule was the same for each of the three cases described in the chapter, and merely altered in substance. Readers may wish to use this schedule for analysing their own cases.

Appendices: II

The social inquiry reports, which were presented in the four selected cases and described in detail in the goal-setting chapter, are attached below:

A   Probation intervention not indicated—social services involved (2)
B   Social work intervention indicated—high need (4)
C   Intervention through institutional provision indicated (5)
D   Inappropriateness of an institutional sentence indicated (6)

A Probation Intervention not Indicated—Social Services Involved (2)

Report to Oldbridge City Magistrates Court on 3rd June 1975

Relating to: Frances Chivers   (22)   Born: 2.30.53
                18 Mundesley Street
                Oldbridge

Offence

Assault occasioning actual bodily harm.

Previous court appearances

June 1968. Juvenile Court, Oldbridge, Larceny. Committed to Approved School.

Family background

Mrs Chivers was born in Oldbridge, and is one of a family of twelve children. When she was eleven years old her mother died and soon afterwards her father married again. Mrs Chivers states that she had never had a good relationship with her stepmother. Since her own marriage, she has had only limited contact with her family.

When the period in the approved school was completed Mrs Chivers found employment in the north, but was compelled to leave when she became pregnant. She returned to Oldbridge where her baby was born. At eighteen years of age she married Mr Chivers whom she had known since she was a school girl. Although he was not the father of her child, he accepted the baby who was spastic. Unfortunately the baby died at just under a year old. Mr and Mrs Chivers now have two children, one aged two years and one of eight months.

Since their marriage Mr and Mrs Chivers have lived at a number of addresses in the city. At first they lived with the husband's parents. Currently they are living in an old terraced house in an area which is gradually being demolished ready for redevelopment. Mrs Chivers has no idea when the family will be offered other accommodation. The material conditions of the home are poor. The rent for the house is said to be £2.53 per week; in addition there are rent arrears amounting to £17.

Circumstances of the offence

This offence involves an assault by Mrs Chivers on her sister-in-law Mrs Davies. The latter had been living with the Chivers family until the day before this assault took place. Mrs Davies had been asked to leave the house as a result of differences between her and Mrs Chivers. Coinciding with this event the police called at 18 Mundesley Street in order to investigate anonymous allegations that Mrs Chivers was neglecting her children. Mrs Chivers had reason to assume that her sister-in-law was responsible for this and threatened Mrs Davies of the consequences if she were to reappear at their house. Later Mrs Davies called at the home and was assaulted by Mrs Chivers in the street, when other people were present and witnessed the incident.

General

During the preparation of this report Mrs Chivers was extremely co-operative. She showed considerable anxiety about the possible outcome of the court proceedings. The clear and unmistakable impression obtained was that this incident was basically a family dispute and that it must be seen in that context. Mrs Chivers does not hide the fact that there have been difficulties between her and various members of her husband's large family. Furthermore this assault appears to have been the result of some provocation. Since the incident Mrs Chivers and Mrs Davies have seen each other, without further arguments or unpleasantness.

Mrs Chivers impresses as a fairly straightforward young woman who felt justified in the action she took on the occasion of the assault. She thinks that the incident has now been enlarged out of all proportion. There is little to suggest that she is frequently involved in similar incidents with friends. Clearly her life has not been without difficulties but, fortunately, her marriage remains stable.

Mrs Chivers's children have suffered from some degree of ill health and her standards of care and cleanliness may not be as high as would be desired. Mrs Chivers is, however, in regular contact with a social worker and it is not felt that any additional form of supervision is indicated.

Mrs Chivers is not in employment and at the time of preparation of this report her husband has been dismissed from his job following a series of apparently unavoidable absences. To date he has made no claim for social security and he hopes to obtain work soon. In the circumstances, it does not seem that Mrs Chivers is in a position to meet any financial penalty.

Conclusion

Because of the facts surrounding this offence and as Mrs Chivers is already in contact with a social worker, it is suggested that this matter be dealt with by means of a conditional discharge.

(Signed) A. N. Tompkin
Probation Officer

B Social Work Intervention Indicated—High Need (4)

Report to Sandford City Magistrates Court on 15th May 1975

Relating to: 1 Marguerite Mayhew   (24)   Born 22.2.51
             123 Stuart Avenue
       2 Simon Mayhew   (21)   Born 11.2.54

Offence

Jointly did steal packet of bacon, ½lb cheese and ½lb butter, together valued at £1.15p.

Previous

Marguerite Mayhew

1   20.5.67   Sandford Juvenile Court. Assault O.A.B.H. Fit Person Order.

2 11.2.68 Sandford Magistrates' Court. Larceny. Probation
Order, 2 years. Condition of Residence 12 Months.
3 27.6.70 Northfield Magistrates' Court. Probation, 2 years.

Simon Mayhew

None known

Home Circumstances

This couple live in a two-bedroomed flat for which they pay £6.95
per week. Conditions are clean and comfortable.

Personal histories

Marguerite

Eight years ago enquiries were made by this department for the
juvenile court relating to Marguerite which resulted in a Fit Person
Order being made. The information collected about the circumstances at that time was full and detailed and was available to me for
this inquiry. The reports made for and during a probation order with
a condition of residence were also considered by me. During the
period of the probation order Marguerite's attitude changed for the
better; she made good use of supervision and matured considerably.
Following a further court appearance in 1970, when a two year
probation order was made, no further background information is
obtainable. It appears that the order expired normally.

As a child Marguerite experienced serious domestic disruptions.
These led to her living with her grandmother for eighteen months,
and finally she was taken into care. She has a good ability (IQ 128)
and she attended Foulton grammar school. There she obtained 2 'O'
levels.

During the current inquiry, Marguerite has been co-operative. She
is clearly worried about the outcome of the court hearing. Subsequent to the offence she was referred by the Samaritans to the
Heights Psychiatric Hospital. She stayed for two days before taking
her own discharge.

Simon

A relaxed, placid young man of previous good character. He has
been a calming influence during the early stages of this inquiry.

Two visits to the home have been made and Marguerite and
Simon have been seen at the office. On each occasion they have been
most co-operative. Initially Marguerite was very anxious and agitated.
She became calmer when she was able to see that I needed

178

knowledge of their circumstances to be able to provide helpful information to the court.

In discussion about events surrounding the offence, the couple revealed that they have a large number of debts, including an electricity bill for £64.55. They were trying to pay various bills from their wages in order of priority. At the time of the offence they were without money and they say that they felt desperate.

Simon is working near the home at the hosiery firm, Brownford Ltd. He is employed as a packer and earns £31.10 per week. Marguerite has just begun work in a part-time capacity. She earns 67p an hour for a 32½ hour week. There has been further alleviation of their financial position during the inquiry period as they have received an outstanding tax rebate of £55. This will help them pay the electricity bill.

The couple have been married since last September and they are still experiencing the difficulties of setting up a home. Their reasonable attitude towards me makes me optimistic, that if the court feels that supervision could be helpful, that I would receive every co-operation. Marguerite's periodic spells of depression show that she and Simon need considerable support.

(Signed) J. P. Swallow

C Intervention through Institutional Provision Indicated (5)

Report to Crown Court sitting at Newton—January 1975

Regarding: Arthur James Finder   (17)   Born 9.10.57
46 Dewsbury Street,
Newton

Charges

1   Theft of cash box containing £198.98.
2   Theft of handbag and contents valued at £133.00.
It is understood that Finder is asking for about 90 other similar offences to be considered, and that additional charges might also be made.

Previous

3.11.74   Newton Magistrates Court. Theft. Probation Order
2 years
Theft. Fined £18
5.11.74   Newton Juvenile Court. Theft (1 TIC) Attendance
Centre 24 hours

Family background and circumstances

Finder's home is a well-kept council house on the Fullwood Estate. He lives with his paternal grandmother and his younger brother, Philip, aged 15. The two boys have lived with their grandparents since infancy. When their father was with the services in Cyprus, their mother left them in the care of her husband's parents and returned to her home in another region. The mother did not return and Mr and Mrs Finder senior continued to look after them. It is believed that their mother is now in a psychiatric hospital. Their father obtained a divorce, and has since married again. He and his second wife have three children and the family live in another part of the same council estate containing his parents' home. Two years ago the grandfather died suddenly.

Family relationships

The relationship between Finder and his grandparents has been almost the same as a parent-child relationship. By the time he was five he knew that his natural parents were not the people who looked after him. He seems to have accepted this fact without difficulty.

The grandmother has a very warm approach to both the grandsons. She states that there have been no unusual or particular behaviour problems during their upbringing. Mrs Finder senior looks upon them very much as her own sons. She had found it specially satisfying to be able to care for them, for to some extent it made up for the death of one of her own sons. This had occurred just before the two children were left by their mother.

From information obtained, the grandfather until he died two years ago, carried out a normal paternal role. His death deeply affected his wife and was a serious loss to Finder. There is no evidence that the boy had an abnormal reaction to this event at the time.

Since the mother left the children Finder has had little contact with her, and she seems to have little significance in their thinking. The relationship he has with his father is a fairly casual one, not unlike that between uncle and nephew. Over the years, Mr Finder has become involved with his second family and has been happy to leave the upbringing of the two boys in his mother's hands. The situation is an unusual one but there are no signs of rejection apparent and Mr Finder retains some feeling of responsibility for his son, particularly since the death of the grandfather.

Education

Finder attended the Piper Road Infant and Royal Avenue Junior schools, before moving to Grasmount Secondary school. It seems that he had a good school career; he was encouraged to work

180

towards CSE examinations. The death of his grandfather, however, led him to think he should take some responsibility for his grandmother. This affected his decision about school and he chose to leave and find work.

Work

After school he was apprenticed to Una Paint Ltd., decorating contractors. After about six months he left in order to earn a higher wage and moved then to work in a factory, manufacturing clothing with A. B. Black and Sons. The change from the apprenticeship seems to have been the start of an unsettled period of work for Finder. He soon left Black's and moved to another firm for a short time before returning to Black's. About three months ago he sustained an arm injury when playing football. His job did not remain open to him during his absence of several weeks and he has continued to be unemployed since then.

The offences

Finder appeared at courts on 3 and 5 November for offences which were part of a number of similar 'walk-in' thefts which he has now admitted. It seems that these offences started when he was looking for work and he took the opportunity to steal unattended articles from business premises which he visited in the course of his enquiries about employment. The fact that a large number of similar thefts were carried out indicates that Finder and his co-defendants quickly found these excursions lucrative.

Personality

Finder is not without intelligence and he has a polite and co-operative disposition. The unusual background circumstances appear not to have affected his development unduly. This could be because of the early age at which he came into the care of his grandparents and because they were open with him and informed him appropriately about the situation.

The grandfather's death might, however, be linked with Finder's current difficulties. There has been no stabilising influence from an important male figure at a crucial stage of development for this youth. Although he seems not to have acquired completely antisocial and unacceptable values, he has, it would seem, suffered from this lack of a father figure in the home, at the stage which involves taking on responsibilities of employment and of being an adult. He allowed his employment situation to deteriorate; he kept the company of other unemployed young men and failed to continue to behave in a trouble-free manner.

Response to supervision

Soon after the probation order was made on 3 November the larger number of offences began to come to light. During the period since the order was made Finder has kept appointments with the probation officer, but he has not found work. It seems that he was not optimistic about the outcome of a further court appearance and because he thought a custodial sentence likely, he made no serious effort to find employment. It is now believed that he will be facing further charges for offences which have been carried out since the probation order was made.

Summary and conclusion

There are some regrettable features in the picture that this young man's circumstances present. Until recently he had never been accused of law breaking. His activities of a criminal nature, however, have been over a period on a large scale. They seem to indicate a drift into crime which has arisen because of lack of purpose in a deteriorated employment situation, rather than because he has developed an openly hostile attitude to other people in the community.

Finder needs guidance from a male authority figure who could engage and help him to return to a regular working routine. In view of the number of serious offences and his lack of effort during the short period of probation, it could be that it will be thought necessary for him to experience a period in a custodial setting before such measures can be taken on his behalf.

(Signed) Michael Stitchem
Probation officer

D Inappropriateness of an Institutional Sentence Indicated (6)

Report to the Bridgetown Juvenile Court on 13th March 1978

Regarding: Christopher Blenkin   (15)   D.O.B. 16.8.62.
15 Snows Lane
Bridgetown

Offence

Assault occasioning actual bodily harm.
1 Today's alleged offence took place at school following an argument with a fellow pupil. Christopher states that the other boy referred to him not having a father, at which point Christopher lost

his temper. He states that he acted in self-defence by hitting the boy.

2   Christopher is the eldest of three children. His parents are local people and were divorced four years ago. The family home, a privately owned semi-detached house is still jointly owned by the parents. Until recently Christopher lived there with his mother and younger brother and sister. Mr Blenkin visits the home regularly to see the children, but there is often friction between the parents on these visits, and this has been reflected in Christopher's behaviour at home. Since I have known the family there has been a consistent deterioration in the relationship between Christopher and his mother. He has made no secret of the fact that he wanted to live with his father. During this period Christopher has adopted a sullen and unco-operative manner with all adults except Mr Blenkin. Thus he has caused behaviour problems at home, at school and on occasions he has been difficult to handle in the intermediate treatment group of which he is a member.

3   Mrs Blenkin suffers from rheumatoid arthritis and has found Christopher difficult to manage and she has felt almost powerless to influence his behaviour. The boy's first offence of assault arose from a domestic upset when Mrs Blenkin had called in the police to help her; the recent offence occurred during a period when he had been suspended from school because of his unruly behaviour. The present matter can also be seen in the context of the frustration felt by this highly volatile youngster because of dissatisfaction with his domestic life. In December last Mrs Blenkin sought help from the social services department because she felt she could cope no longer with Christopher and he had been placed on a waiting list for voluntary reception into care. Mr Blenkin then again became more prominent in his son's life, and with encouragement from the school, the social services department and from me, the father set up arrangements to provide a home for Christopher and himself. He achieved this a few days ago, following his recent marriage.

4   Christopher's difficult behaviour goes back several years, probably exacerbated by the family problems. There has emerged a pattern of truculence and defiance in his mother's home and at school. He seems to have few friends and spends much of his time alone at home. The move to Mr Blenkin's home has occurred at a crucial point for Christopher as it seemed that he would inevitably be taken into some kind of institutional care. The outcome of the move to his father's home has yet to be seen, but every support will be offered to help him settle to his new circumstances and to change his behaviour pattern of recent years. It has been difficult so far to work with Mr Blenkin because his response to probation officers and others in authority tends to be defensive, and again this is mirrored by Christopher. In the remainder of the supervision period

there may be some difficulty in establishing a proper basis of co-operation, although there appears to be no difference of opinion with Mr Blenkin's view of the help that his son needs. In the last few months Mrs Blenkin has been physically and mentally exhausted by the pressures created by Christopher. She is currently anxiously sceptical about how complete his recent move will prove to be.

5   Christopher is a pupil at Fourways Community College until the summer and he is unlikely to change for his final term. I have regular contact with the staff and know that they would like to help Christopher negotiate his last school term in the way least painful to all concerned. The head has sought the father's co-operation in this. At present Christopher has just completed a further period of suspension.

6   Christopher has attended a six month programme of an intermediate treatment group and this will be completed in two weeks. The benefits which he may have gained here tended to be overshadowed by the anxieties in his domestic situation.

7   It has been difficult to talk to Christopher, at any depth, about this offence but this is found to be the same with most subjects. He is a boy who contains a lot of his feelings, and gives the impression of being very tense and emotionally brittle.

8   There is a clear need for continued supervision; this is characterised currently by volatile feelings all round, and at the same time Christopher is subject to considerable change. This change is welcome but needs to be channelled carefully if it is to succeed. There are many imponderables about Christopher's future, but if he can negotiate the domestic change and the move from school to work without too many disruptions, he may be able to consolidate for the first time for several years.

9   The present offence occurred before Christopher's last court appearance when he was ordered to the Attendance Centre. His overt violence is a worrying aspect of his behaviour. I consider it to be linked to his inner frustrations and that it is not likely to be affected by the punitive or deterrent powers of the court. It is more likely to be eradicated by establishing him in a home and work setting where these frustrations are lessened. Whilst holding this view, I also consider that today a financial penalty would be appropriate as it would register on a limited level, the disapproval of the court and of society towards this kind of behaviour. Christopher has part-time work for which he earns several pounds a week, so he would be expected to pay any financial penalty imposed by the court. The supervision order remains in force until August.

Charles White
Probation and After-care Officer
March 1978.

Bibliography

Aubert, V. (1963), 'Conscientious objectors before Norwegian military courts', in Schubert, G., ed., *Judicial Decision-making*, New York, Free Press, pp. 201-19.

Baker, R. (1975), 'Toward generic social work practice—a review and some innovations', *British Journal of Social Work*, 5(2), pp. 193-215.

Bartlett, H. M. (1970), *The Common Base of Social Work Practice*, New York, National Association of Social Work.

Bean, P. (1975a), 'Social inquiry reports—a recommendation for disposal', Part I, *Justice of the Peace*, 11 October, vol. 139, No. 41, pp. 568-9.

Bean P. (1975b), 'Social inquiry reports—a recommendation for disposal', Part II, *Justice of the Peace*, 18 October, vol. 139, No. 42, pp. 585-7.

Bean, P. (1976), *Rehabilitation and Deviance*, London, Routledge & Kegan Paul.

Bernstein, B. (1971), *Class, Codes and Control: Theoretical Studies Towards a Sociology of Language*, vol. I, London, Routledge & Kegan Paul.

Biestek, F. (1961), *The Casework Relationship*, London, Allen & Unwin.

Bottoms, A. E. (1974), 'On the decriminalisation of English juvenile courts', in Hood, R., ed., *Crime, Criminology and Public Policy*, London, Heinemann, pp. 319-45.

Box, S. and Forde, J. (1971), 'The facts don't fit: on the relationship between social class and criminal behaviour', *Sociological Review*, 19 (1), pp. 31-52.

Brennan, W. C. (1973), 'The practitioner as theoretician', *Education for Social Work*, 9 (2), pp. 5-12.

Briar, S. and Miller, H. (1971), *Problems and Issues in Social Casework*, New York, Columbia University Press.

Butrym, Z. (1976), *The Nature of Social Work*, London, Macmillan.

Caplan, G. (1961), *An Approach to Community Mental Health*, London, Tavistock.

Cicourel, A. (1964), *Method and Measurement in Sociology*, New York, Free Press.

Coates, L. V. (1978), 'A framework for differential assessment in Probation', (mimeo).

Bibliography

Cohen, S. (1975), 'It's all right for you to talk: political and sociological manifestos for social action', in Bailey, R. and Brake, M. *Radical Social Work*, London, Arnold, pp. 76-95.

Colwell Report, (1974), Report of the committee of inquiry into the care and supervision provided by local authorities and other agencies in relation to Maria Colwell and the co-ordination between them, London, HMSO.

Compton, B. R. and Galaway, B. (1975), *Social Work Processes*, Illinois, Dorsey Press.

Corrigan, P., and Leonard, P. (1978), *Social Work Practice under Capitalism: A Marxist Approach*, London, Macmillan.

Cross, C. P., ed., (1974), *Interviewing and Communication in Social Work*, London, Routledge & Kegan Paul.

Davies, M. (1971), 'Social enquiry for the courts: an examination of the current position in England and Wales' (mimeo), Paper read at the Anglo-Scandinavian Research Seminar in Criminology, Norway.

Davies, M. (1973), *An Index of Social environment*, London, HMSO.

Davies, M. (1974), 'Social inquiry for the courts', *British Journal of Criminology*, 14(1), pp. 18-33.

Davies, M. and Sinclair, I.A.C. (1971), 'Families, hostels and delinquents: an attempt to assess cause and effect', *British Journal of Criminology*, 11(3), pp. 213-29.

Dobson, G. (1976), 'The differential treatment unit', Part I. *Probation Journal*, 23, pp. 105-8.

Evans, R. (1976), 'Some implications of an integrated model for social work theory and practice', *British Journal of Social Work*, 6(2), pp. 177-200.

Evans, R. and Webb, D. (1977), 'Sociology and social work practice: explanation or method', *Contemporary Social Work Education*, 1(2), pp. 15-26.

Evans, R. and Webb, D. (1978), 'Developing a client-centred sociology', *Community Care*, 22, pp. 20-2.

Ferard, M. L. and Hunnybun, N. K. (1962), *The Caseworker's Use of Relationships*, London, Tavistock Publications.

Ford, P. (1972), *Advising Sentencers: A Study of Recommendations made by Probation Officers to the Courts*, Oxford, Blackwell.

Forder, A. and Kay, S. (1973), 'Social work', in Cooper, M.H. (ed), *Social Policy: A Survey of Recent Developments*, Oxford, Blackwell, pp. 1-44.

Foster, Z. P. (1973), 'How social work can influence hospital management of fatal illness', in Pincus, A. and Minahan, A., *Social Work Practice: Model and Method*, Illinois, Peacock, pp. 300-8.

Goldstein, H. (1973), *Social Work Practice: A Unitary Approach*, Columbia, University of South Carolina Press.

Haines, J. (1975), *Skills and Methods in Social Work*, London, Constable.

Handler, J. (1973), *The Coercive Social Worker*, Chicago, Rand McNally.

Hardiker, P. (1972), 'Problem-definition: an interactionist approach, in Jehu, *et al.*, *Behavioural Modification in Social Work*, London, Wiley, pp. 99-125.

Hardiker, P. (1975), *Ideologies in Social Inquiry Reports*, Research Report, Social Science Research Council.

Hardiker, P. (1976), 'Images of deviants', *New Society*, 37(717), pp. 15-16.

Hardiker, P. (1977a), 'Social work ideologies in the probation service', *British Journal of Social Work*, 7(2), pp. 131-54.

Hardiker, P. (1977b), *A Probation Intake Team in Action*, Research Report, Leicestershire Probation and After Care Service, and Social Science Research Council.

Hardiker, P. (1978), 'The role of probation officers in sentencing', in Parker H. ed., *Social Work and the Court*, London, Arnold.

Hardiker, P. and Webb, D. (1978), 'Explaining deviant behaviour: the social context of action and infraction accounts in the probation service', *Sociology*, vol. 13, No. 1, January 1979.

Heinler, E. (1975), *Survival in Society*, London, Weidenfeld & Nicolson.

Herbert, M. (1978), *Conduct Disorders of Childhood and Adolescence*, Chichester, Wiley.

Hofstad, M. O. (1977), 'Treatment in a juvenile court setting', in Reid, W. J. and Epstein, L., eds, *Task-Centred Practice*, New York, Columbia University Press, PP. 195-201.

Holgate, E. (ed.) (1972), *Communicating with Children*, London, Longman.

Hollis, F. (1965), *Casework: A Psychosocial Therapy* (Second edition 1972). New York, Random House.

Home Office Circular 188/1968—*Social Enquiry Reports Before Sentence*.

Home Office Circular 194/1974 to all chief probation officers, 25 October, 1974.

Hutton, J. M. (1977), *Short-term Contracts in Social Work*, London, Routledge & Kegan Paul.

Jarvis, F. V. (1974), *Probation Officers' Manual* (2nd edn), London, Butterworths, pp. 108-39.

Jehu, D. (1964), *Casework before Admission to Care*, London, Association of Child Care Officers Monograph.

Jehu, D. et al. (1972), *Behaviour Modification in Social Work*, London Wiley.

Jordan, W. (1972), *The Social Worker in Family Situations*, London, Routledge & Kegan Paul.

Keith-Lucas, A. (1972), *Giving and Taking Help*, Chapel Hill, University of North Carolina Press.

Kuhn, T. (1970), *The Structure of Scientific Revolution*, University of Chicago Press.

Laing, R. D. (1969), *Intervention in Social Situations*, London, Association of Family Caseworkers.

Leighton, N. (1973), 'The act of understanding', *British Journal of Social Work*, 3(4), pp. 509-24.

Lemert, E. M. (1976), 'Choice and change in juvenile justice', *British Journal of Law and Society*, 3(1), pp. 59-75.

Leonard, P. (1975a), 'Towards a paradigm for radical practice', in Bailey, R. and Brake, M. (eds.), *Radical Social Work*, London, Arnold, pp. 46-61.

Leonard, P. (1975b), 'Explanation and education in social work', *British Journal of Social Work*, 5(3), pp. 325-33.

Lewis, H. (1972), 'Developing a program responsive to new knowledge and values', in, Mullen, E. J. and Dumpson, J. R., eds, *Evaluation of Social Work Intervention*, San Fransisco, Jossey Bass.

McCullough, J. W. and Prins, H. A. (1975), *Signs of Stress*, London, Collins.

McDermott, F. E., ed. (1975), *Self Determination in Social Work*, London, Routledge & Kegan Paul.

Maluccio, A. N. and Marlow, W. D. (1974), 'The case for contract', *Social Work (U.S.)*, 19(1), pp. 28-36.

Manis, J. and Meltzer, B., eds (1967), Symbolic Interaction: *A Reader in Social Psychology*, Boston, Allyn & Bacon.

Mathieson, D. (1975), 'Probation officers, sentencers of the future', *Justice of the Peace*, 22 March, pp. 162-4.

Mathieson, D. (1976), 'The social enquiry report', *Justice of the Peace*, 8 May, pp. 246-8.

Mathieson, D. (1977), 'Social inquiry reports—time to plot a new course', *Justice of the Peace*, 16 April, pp. 224-6.

Mathieson, D. and Herbert, L. (1975), *Reports for Courts*, Surrey, National Association of Probation Officers.

Mathieson, D. A. and Walker, A. J. (1971), *Social Enquiry Reports*, London, National Association of Probation Officers.

Matza, D. (1964), *Delinquency and Drift*, New York, Wiley.

Matza, D. (1969), *Becoming Deviant*, New Jersey, Prentice Hall.

May, D. (1971), 'Delinquency control and the treatment model: some implications of recent legislation', *British Journal of Criminology*, 11(4) pp. 359-70.

Mayer, J. E. and Timms, N. (1970), *The Client Speaks: Working Class Impressions of Casework*, London, Routledge & Kegan Paul.

Mead, G. H. (1934), *Mind, Self and Society*, University of Chicago Press.

Monger, M. (1972), *Casework in Probation*, 2nd Edn., London, Butterworths.

Monger, M. (1974), 'The juvenile court as a casework situation', *Justice of the Peace*, 138(9), 2 March, pp. 123-5.

Morison Report (1962), *Report of the Departmental Committee on the Probation Service*, Cmd 1650, London, HMSO.

Parsloe, P. (1976), 'Social work and the justice model', *British Journal of Social Work*, 6(1), pp. 71-89.

Pearce, I. and Wareham, A. (1977), 'The questionable relevance of research into social inquiry reports', *Howard Journal*, XVI(2), pp. 97-108.

Perlman, H. H. (1956), *Social Casework—A Problem-Solving Process*, Chicago University Press.

Perlman, H. H. (1968), *Persona: Social Role and Personality*, University of Chicago Press.

Perry, F. G. (1974), *Information for the Court—A New Look at Social Inquiry Reports*, Cambridge, Institute of Criminology.

Pincus, A. and Minahan, A. (1973), *Social Work Practice: Model and Method*, Illinois, Peacock Itasca.

Plant, Raymond. (1976), *Social and Moral Theory in Casework*, London, Routledge & Kegan Paul.

Plotnikoff, J. (1973), 'A problem for law and social work: social enquiry reports on people pleading not guilty', *British Journal of Social Work*, 3(2), pp. 175-87.

Popper, K. R. (1963), *Conjectures and Refutations*, London, Routledge & Kegan Paul.

Powers of Criminal Courts Act, Chapter 62 (1973), London, HMSO.

Prins, H. (1973), *Criminal Behaviour: An Introduction to its Study and Treatment*, London, Pitman.

Rein, M. (1970a), 'The crossroads for social work', *Social Work*, 27(4), pp. 18-27.

Rein, M. (1970b), 'Social work in search of a radical profession', *Social Work (US)*, 15(2), pp. 13-28.

Richmond, M. (1917), *Social Diagnosis*, New York, Free Press.

Ripple, L., Alexander, E. and Polemis, B. W. (1964), *Motivation, Capacity and Opportunity. Studies in Casework Theory and Practice*, Chicago, School of Social Service Administration.

Rose, A. (ed.), (1962), *Human Behaviour and Social Processes*, London, Routledge & Kegan Paul.

Ruddock, R. (1969), *Roles and Relationships*, London, Routledge & Kegan Paul.

Sainsbury, E. (1970), *Social Diagnosis in Casework*, London, Routledge & Kegan Paul.

Satir, V. (1967), *Conjoint Family Therapy* (Revised edn), Palo Alto, California, Science & Behaviour Books.

Sheldon, B. (1978), 'Theory and practice in social work: a re-examination of a tenuous relationship', *British Journal of Social Work*, 8(1), pp. 1-22.

Smith, G. (1977), 'The place of "professional ideology" in the analysis of "social policy": some theoretical conclusions from a pilot study of the children's panels', *Sociological Review*, 25(4), pp. 843-65.

Smith, G. and Harris, R. (1972), 'Ideologies of need and the organization of social work departments', *British Journal of Social Work*, 2(1), pp. 27-45.

Specht, H. (1977), 'Theory as a guide to practice', in Specht, H. and Vickery, A., *Integrating Social Work Methods*, London, Allen & Unwin, pp. 28-35.

Statham, D. (1978), *Radicals in Social Work*, London, Routledge & Kegan Paul.

Stevenson, O. (1978), 'Reception into care—a case example illustrating the use of theory in practice', in Central Council for Education and Training in Social Work. Study No. 1., *Good Enough Parenting*, Central Council for Education and Training in Social Work, London, pp. 42-9.

Stoll, C. S. (1968), 'Images of man and social control', *Social Forces*, 47(2), pp. 119-27.

The Streatfeild Report (1961), *Report of the Interdepartmental Committee on the Business of the Criminal Courts*, Cmnd 1289, London, HMSO.

Taylor, I., Walton, P. and Young, J. (1973), *The New Criminology*, London, Routledge & Kegan Paul.

Timms, N. & R. (1977), *Perspectives in Social Work*, London, Routledge & Kegan Paul.

Tod, R. J. N. ed., (1971a), *Social Work in Foster Care*, London, Longmans.

Tod, R. J. N. ed., (1971b), *Social Work in Adoption*, London, Longmans.

Bibliography

Turner, F. J., ed., (1974), *Social Work Treatment: Interlocking Theoretical Approaches,* New York, Free Press.

Vaisey, R. (1976), 'The differential treatment unit, Part II', *Probation Journal,* 23, pp. 108-12.

Walrond-Skinner, S. (1976), *Family Therapy—The Treatment of Natural Systems,* London, Routledge & Kegan Paul.

Waters, R. W. (1976), 'The value of short-term work', *Probation Journal,* 23, pp. 17-20.

Wheeler, S., ed., (1968), *Controlling Delinquents,* New York, Wiley.

Winnicott, C. (1971), *Child Care and Social Work,* London, Bookstall Services.

Yelloly, M. (1972), 'The helping relationship', in Jehu, D., *et al., Behaviour Modification in Social Work*, London, Wiley, pp. 150-60.

Index

aquisition of information, 1, 2, 12, 13, 14, 17, 37, 79, 81, 85, 89, 102-6, 121-30, 135-9, 144, 164, 165, 173; skills and methods in, 18-38

agency setting, 15, 16, 19, 101, 111, 150; records, 1, 19, 20, 21, 89, 178

antecedents, behaviour, consequences (ABC), 121, 122, 151

assessment and intervention distinction, 14, 15, 75-7, 80-1, 83-4, 88, 92, 101, 133, 143, 158, 169; merging, 140, 142, 156-7

assessment model, 16, 101, 161-3, 172

assessment process, viii, 11, 15, 16, 17, 25, 45, 55, 73, 75, 88, 101, 121, 134, 139, 143, 157, 160, 163, 170

at risk register, 103, 106, 113, 125

bail hostel, 16, 65

balance sheet, 3, 57, 74, 77, 82, 86-7, 115, 130, 140, 143, 153, 170; of risk, need and resources, 58-68, 80, 81, 163, 166-7, 169

behaviour modification, 8, 170

behavioural casework, 120, 148, 152; programme, 157

boundary, 15; to assessment role, 168-9; to interview, 19, 29; to investigation, 18, 26, 38, 47, 73, 79, 96, 162, 168; of professional responsibility, 24, 101, 128, 142, 164

care proceedings, 13, 20, 115, 117-18, 178; orders, 14, 91, 153, 155, 156, 167, 168

change agent, viii

child abuse, 111

Children and Young Persons Act (1969), 102; (1975), 118

Child Treatment Research Unit, 17, 101, 120, 129, 132

classical justice, 12, 47, 48, 97

client, role of, 19, 30-1

communication: barriers to, 29, 31-5, 82, 85, 146, 148, 170; in interviews, 29, 90, 146; non-verbal, 15; processes, 163, 164, 169; with children, 27, 28, 132

community home, 16

conceptualisation, 6, 7; process of, 6, 99

conceptualise, 18, 72, 76, 99

contracts, 13, 14, 76, 94-5, 114, 119, 132, 155, 168

crisis intervention, 15, 76, 98; situation, 22, 24-5, 83

cultural factors, 34, 79, 85, 98, 113, 146, 153

custodial sentence, 9, 14, 42, 48, 88, 166, 182

custody, 10, 61-2, 88-9; and access decisions, 19; inevitable, 58-9, 61, 74, 84, 87-8, 93, 95, 97, 98, 99, 167; inquiry, 20, 21-2, 23, 27, 28, 76; interview in, 26

divorce court welfare, 13, 20, 21, 23; case, 19

ethical implications, 133

family therapy, 51

filter diagram of assessment, 169; information, 5, 6, 96, 99, 166;

191

Index

process, 38, 54-5, 98, 172
formulating assessment, 3, 4, 14, 17, 55, 57, 80, 82-3, 86, 91, 99, 101, 130-2, 153-4, 157, 166-7, 169-74; skills and methods in, 57-72
foster care, 105, 106, 109, 115, 119, 155, 156-7
framework(s), ix, 5, 11, 18-19, 37, 40-56, 157; for study, 51-6, 85, 90, 143, 149-53, 162; treatment, 3, 4, 52-3, 79, 99
frequency, intensity, number, duration and sense (FINDS), 121, 122, 149, 151

goal, 3, 4, 15, 19; analysis of, 77-94, 115, 154-6; boundaries to, 94; setting, 13, 14, 17, 73-100, 116-19, 132-3, 139, 140, 142, 154-6, 164, 167-8, 170, 174
guardian ad litem, 13
guidelines in data collection, 23-6

hospital setting, 13, 140, 151
hypothesis building, 20, 22, 26, 121, 146; testing, 21, 37, 106

ideologies, 52-6, 99, 152-3, 157, 166; and practice theory, 55, 99, 152
individualisation, ix, 32, 41, 47, 79, 82, 85, 99, 149, 163, 165-6, 169, 170, 172
information, acquisition of, 1, 2, 12, 13, 14, 17, 18-38, 79, 81, 85, 89, 102-6, 121-30, 135-9, 144, 164-5, 173; in affidavits, 20; client as main source of, 24-5, 28; study of, 12, 13, 38-58, 79, 82, 85, 90, 106-15, 124-30, 148
intake systems, 75, 111; worker, 95, 115, 155
interprofessional confidentiality, 25, 36
interviews aims of, 141; in custody, 26; in data collection, 19; first, 21, 22, 23, 26, 144; guidelines, 23-33, 164; schedule, 173; tape-recorded, 17, 101, 161

justice ideology, 152; issues, 64; model, 47, 167
juvenile(s) court, 1, 22, 89, 113, 118, 175, 177, 178, 179, 182; interviewing, 31; offenders, 13, 15, 25, 27, 28, 43, 50, 63, 76, 182-4

learning theory, 8, 151, 163, 164

model of assessment, 16, 101, 161-3, 172; social work processes, 13
Morison Report (1962), 12, 48, 75, 93

need(s), 3, 4, 15, 57, 59-62, 70, 116, 130-3, 177; balancing risk, resources, 65-8, 153-4, 166-7
non-accidental injury, 17, 20, 26, 28-9, 101, 107, 111, 144, 165
not guilty plea, 49, 93

paradigm, 40, 170-2
personality, as a factor, 127
place of safety order, 104-5, 111, 115, 117, 119, 144, 155, 156
plans, long-term, 14, 81, 94; treatment, 14, 155
Powers of the Criminal Courts Act (1973), 11, 48
practice theory, ix, x, 38, 40, 69, 71, 95, 96, 98-100, 101, 143, 163, 169-70, 172; and ideologies, 55-6; and social inquiry assessments, 1-17, 71, 96; and theory of practice, 5-11, 71-2, 98-100, 158, 159, 169, 170
pre-trial inquiries, 49, 50, 76
previous criminal record, 2, 18, 39, 40, 41-2, 61, 66, 74
principles of practice, 11, 96, 144
probation officer styles, 50-1
problem(s) behavioural, 120-32, 145, 180, 183; definition, 15; emotional, 16; financial, 3, 45, 79; personal, 2, 5, 12, 39, 44, 53
process of assessment, viii, 11, 15, 16, 17, 25, 45, 55, 73, 75, 88, 101, 121, 134, 139, 143, 157, 160-3, 170; of conceptualisation, 6, 99; of helping, 13; of phases, 13, 14; of using knowledge, 11, 13, 15, 72, 152, 159-61, 170
processes, social work, 13, 15, 18, 35, 75, 88, 93
psycho-dynamic casework, 5, 6, 7, 8; explanations, 8, 38, 47, 51, 54, 55, 143; theories, 9, 15, 75, 99, 164
psycho-social perspective, 38, 148, 170-1

recommendations, definition of, 73
records, agency, 1, 19, 20, 21; and legal documents, 20; previous, 25, 178

referral issue, 18, 19, 21, 22, 42, 55, 103, 110, 114, 120-1, 134, 149, 165, 166, 173
relationship casework, 14; purposeful, 9, 18; social work, 15, 23, 33, 55, 75, 119, 133, 156
reports, use of, 96-8; presentation of, 168
resource(s), 3, 4, 18, 33, 44, 48, 49-50, 57, 62-8, 70, 115, 131, 137, 153-4, 165; and agency function, 49-50, 51, 77; factor, 140
risk, 3, 4, 57, 58-9, 65-9, 84, 116, 117, 130, 153-4, 166

sentencing policy, 18, 40, 47-9, 51, 57, 74, 113; document, 50
settings, different, 16, 17, 101-58; hospital, 13; interview, 26; organisational, 18, 75
skills and methods in acquisition of information, 18-38; formulating assessments, 57-72; setting goals, 73-100; social work, viii, 5, 19, 35; study of information, 39-56; in writing reports, 96
social control factors, 47-51, 57, 99, 150
social inquiry writer, 11; writing, 96
social learning theory, 127
social science theory, 11, 21, 55, 71, 98, 144, 152, 159, 164
social services, 13, 17, 49, 63, 78-9, 98, 101, 102, 113, 125, 132, 175, 183
social work assessments, 101-58; and social inquiry reports, 11-16

social work principles, 13, 16, 36, 37, 96; processes, 13, 15, 18, 35, 75, 88, 93; theories, 14, 21, 151
sociological theories, 9, 52, 98, 170; project, 16, 72, 159
sociology, 8, 151
stereotype, 22, 32-3
strategic report, 74
Streatfeild Report (1961), 12, 47, 75, 96
stress factors, 8, 21, 40, 46-7, 59, 79, 82, 86, 90, 103, 111, 112, 149; situations, 15, 19
study of factors, 10, 13, 14, 17, 39, 79, 82, 85, 90, 107-14, 121-30, 135-40, 148-9, 173; information, 39-56, 79, 82, 85, 90, 106-15, 124-30, 166

tape-recorded interview(s), 17, 101, 161
tariff in reverse, 69-72, 153; sentence, 12, 59, 78, 79, 92, 97
task-centred work, 15
terminally-ill patient, 17, 134-54, 156, 157, 170
theories, as explanations, 163-70
theory of practice and practice theory, 5-11, 71-2, 98-100, 158, 159, 169, 170
treatment model, 9, 92, 99; ideology, 166; orientated, 11, 79, 83, 91

worker, role of, 19, 30-1, 74, 80-1, 85, 97, 109, 110, 119, 141, 145, 155, 167